CANNABIS
CULTIVATOR

CANNABIS CULTIVATOR

A STEP-BY-STEP GUIDE TO GROWING MARIJUANA

JEFF DITCHFIELD

COLLINS & BROWN

Produced by Collins & Brown
151 Freston Road
London
W10 6TH

An imprint of Anova Books Company Ltd

Copyright © Collins & Brown Limited 2007
Text copyright © Jeff Ditchfield 2006
Text copyright © for pages 100–109 Nick Jones 2003 and
Tim Pilcher 2004; for pages 10–12, 16–20 Tim Pilcher
2004

ISBN-13: 978-1-84340-380-7
ISBN-10: 1-84340-380-3

A CIP catalogue record for this book is available from the
British Library

10 9 8 7 6 5 4 3 2 1

Reproduction by Anorax Ltd, UK
Printed and bound in Taiwan

This book contains information about
Cannabis. Cannabis is a controlled
substance in the United States and other
parts of the world and the use, cultivation,
supply and possession of Cannabis can
carry severe legal penalties.
This book is intended for illustrative and
entertainment purposes only. The
Publisher does not condone the use of
controlled substances and does not
encourage you to break the law.

The Publisher makes no warranties or
representations of any kind in respect of
the accuracy or suitability of the
information contained in this book. The
Publishers shall not be liable for any
direct, indirect or consequential damages
whatsoever resulting from the information
contained in this book.

CONTENTS

INTRODUCTION

I became interested in the medicinal application of cannabis after discovering that a close friend used it to combat the symptoms of her Multiple Sclerosis. I realized that many people could benefit from using cannabis in this way and so I co-founded a medicinal cannabis organization, Bud Buddies, which, on receipt of a recommendation from a doctor, assisted seriously ill people with cannabis and cannabis preparations.

As the medical world became aware of the work of Bud Buddies, I was invited to speak at John Moores University (Liverpool) and at the Royal College of General Practitioners (London) on cannabis cultivation and its medicinal application. Academic studies throughout the world reported many positive results from the use of medicinal cannabis. However, its legal status remained unchanged and, in 2005, the UK Court of Appeal ruled that medical necessity could no longer be used as a defense for its cultivation and usage. This debate continues.

My author's fee has been donated to www.uk420.com in thanks for their collaboration in the writing of this book.

1

SAY HIGH
TO MARY JANE

A POTTED HISTORY

In a Chinese archeological dig at the beginning of 2005 fragments of a small clay beaker were found, quite unremarkable in its design apart from some cannabis twine that had been used to decorate it. The beaker was dated at approximately 10,000 years old.

Cannabis was used throughout the world for medicinal and religious purposes before the beginning of recorded history. In fact, recorded history itself owes a great debt to the invention of hemp paper. Ancient Chinese and Arabic medical texts speak of the use of cannabis in many forms being used to treat a variety of ailments including malaria, insomnia, constipation, and rheumatism. Ancient Chinese medical books also speak of its religious use. The *Pên Ching* states "if one takes it over a long period of time one can communicate with the spirits and one's own body becomes light."

From its earliest beginnings in what would now be Northern China, the Afghan mountains, and Siberia, cannabis spread through the Asian continent and into the Middle East and Africa. It was used to make medicines and parchment but also clothing, ropes, tents, seed for food, and fodder for the livestock. The holy men of many religions noted the temporal "high" that was induced by consuming or inhaling the smoke of the

Two Russian women harvesting a hemp crop in the 1950s. Cannabis has been cultivated in one form or another for thousands of years.

seeds and flowering buds and cannabis became used widely in Taoism and Islam. The Hindus revered the plant so much that Shiva is also called "Lord of Bhang," bhang being the Hindi name for a cannabis-based drink. Early Hebrews, from the time of Christ, used cannabis in the Holy Anointing oil given to Moses.

As early as 2,000 years before Christ the peoples of Eastern Europe and the Russian Steppes can be proven to have been smoking cannabis. Too many references to mention litter ancient Greek and Roman literature, and hieroglyphs of Egypt. Cannabis pollen was discovered on the mummified body of Rameses II and hemp garments and rope in the earlier tomb of Amenophis IV.

Although it was farmed by Anglo-Saxons, charred hemp seeds found in archeological digs in the Northern Isles show that the first cannabis use in the UK was by early settlers who crossed from Europe before the seas rose and the UK became islands. Both Henry VIII and Elizabeth I introduced laws commanding landowners to set aside part of their land to the growing of cannabis hemp for the use of the Navy in sail and rigging. Henry VIII also put into law the "Herbalist Charter," which allowed any common man to share and use medicinal herbs of any kind.

Among the items thought to be essential in building a new nation by the Pilgrim Fathers in their voyage aboard the

Mayflower were bags of cannabis hemp seed. Many of the early states followed the English example and brought in laws instructing that landowners must grow cannabis hemp. People could pay their taxes with cannabis hemp and in Virginia between 1763 and 1767 you could be jailed for not growing it.

Up to the beginning of the 20th century humans greatly benefitted from the use of cannabis. This ended when one man made one speech. The Egyptian delegate at the 1925 League of Nations meeting delivered a tirade against cannabis and pleaded for it to be added to the list of banned drugs in the Hague Convention. Legislation was passed and trading of cannabis resin internationally became illegal worldwide. The 1961 United Nations Single Convention on Narcotics saw the plant join the resin, leaving us with the situation we have today. In some countries a blind eye is turned or medical use may be allowed, but because of one man and one speech cannabis can no longer help humans to grow.

LEGALITY AND HARM

The origins of cannabis prohibition can be traced back to the 1930s when a vigorous campaign was launched by the US Federal Bureau of Narcotics (headed by Harry Anslinger), which portrayed cannabis as a potent narcotic inextricably linked to deviant behavior. The use of cannabis, or to use the term of the time "Reefer Madness," was deemed to lead to violent crime, heroin addiction, social menace, and death.

Cannabis was used as a scapegoat for the ills of American society in films such as Reefer Madness, essentially a government propaganda broadcast.

The World Health Organization's cannabis report of 1955 said: "under the influence of cannabis, the danger of committing unpremeditated murder is very great; it can happen in cold blood, without any reason or motive, unexpectedly, without any preceding quarrel, often the murderer does not even know the victim, and simply kills for pleasure." Six years later cannabis was prohibited internationally under the first United Nations Drug Convention.

Today, most people would consider these views to be extreme.

Worldwide, cannabis is the most widely consumed illicit drug, with an estimated 146 million users. These figures have remained unchanged since the first World Drug Report in 1997.

A VERSATILE PLANT

Cannabis has grown wild across the planet since before man, and has been cultivated since the dawn of the earliest civilizations. Cannabis's varied uses are almost without limit. It is possibly the most versatile and useful plant in existence.

Originally it was used for livestock feed, and to a lesser extent food for humans. Hemp seed's proteins resemble proteins in human blood, making them easier to digest, and they contain essential fatty acids with almost no saturated fat. Just one handful of seeds,

Filipino hempfibre ready for export. Hemp remains a key crop in many parts of the world.

eaten daily, will provide the adequate dose of proteins and essential oils an adult human needs.

When cannabis seeds are crushed they secrete an oil very similar to linseed oil, and this was used to make paints and varnishes until petrochemicals were introduced in the late 1930s. Hemp seed oil was also the world's principal source of combustible oil for lamps until the early 1800s, when it was overtaken by whale oil and then by kerosene in the late 1850s.

The plant can also be used for weaving textiles and was heavily used in the construction of ships' canvas sails, sealant, rope, rugs, carpets, and drapes.

Hemp was also one of the first plants to be used for making paper, and is far more economical than wood, as one acre of hemp could be used to make the same amount of paper as four acres of trees. Until it was generally outlawed around the globe in the first half of the 20th century, the hemp industry was responsible for the vast majority of the world's paper and cloth, with 80 per cent coming from Russia between 1740 and 1940.

Desperate not to become a slave to large oil corporations, car manufacturer Henry Ford realized that fossil fuels could be replaced by a renewable fuel source, like hemp, which can be converted to make methane, methanol or petrol (gasoline) at a fraction of the cost using coal, oil or natural gas. In 1941 Ford even constructed a working automobile entirely from hemp compounds, which was strong enough to withstand a blow from a crowbar.

THE MAJOR VARIETIES

Swedish botanist Carolus Linnaeus first classified the wild plant as *Cannabis sativa* in 1753 while in the Himalayan foothills of India. He believed it was the sole specimen of the genus, a monotypic species. However, in the East Indies in 1785 Jean Baptiste de Lamarck, a French biologist, discovered and named a second species, *Cannabis indica*. It wasn't for

another 139 years that a third type was discovered. In 1924 the botanist D.E. Janischevsky categorized the least-known, *Cannabis ruderalis*, in southeast Russia.

C. sativa grows very tall and loosely branched, whereas *C. indica* is smaller, more conical or pyramidal in shape, and has denser branches. *C. ruderalis* is also small, but has less branches. Of the three, *C. indica* tends to be the most popular; however, there are many strains that now exist that have been cross-bred between *C. indica* and *C. sativa*. *C. ruderalis* is usually used for making cloth, paper and so on, and has had the moniker "industrial hemp" stuck to it.

The cannabis plant is a hardy annual that requires little space, grows well almost anywhere and requires no pesticides.

Marijuana's roots reach deep into the soil, and growing plants in the same soil for 20 years has shown little or no depreciation in the soil quality, unlike, for example, peanuts, which can completely destroy a soil's nutrient content if over-farmed. As cannabis leaves fall and decompose on the soil, they return essential nitrogen and minerals, which are beneficial for the soil and plant. Even the process of treating the stalks and branches of the plant, to prepare it for pulping, returns essential nutrients to the earth, instead of using harmful chemicals that pollute the land.

CHEMICAL ELEMENTS

Cannabis is dioecious, meaning it comes as separate male and female plants. It's important to separate the sexes as early as possible in order to get the best harvest. The male plants are taller, skinnier and have flower-like pods which contain the fertilizing, pollen-generating anthers. The female plant is darker, shorter and generally more squat, and also has short hairs protruding at the end of bracteole pods.

Cannabis is the only plant to contain the chemical elements known as cannabinoids. Almost 40 cannabinoids have been discovered and isolated so far. The most well-known is Delta 9-Tetrahydracannabinol ($C21H30O2$). All cannabis contains at least some Delta 9-THC, although industrial hemp contains only minute traces. Most home-grown cannabis contains much more, with some plants made up of 25 per cent Delta 9-THC.

The second most popular cannabinoid is Delta 9-THC's weaker cousin, Delta 8-THC, which is usually present in very low concentrations, and so the majority of herbal horticulturists and researchers ignore this compound and concentrate on the more potent Delta 9-THC.

Cannabidiol, also known as CBD, appears in nearly all forms of cannabis in varying degrees. Cannabinol is produced as THC oxidizes or degrades.

Only trace amounts appear in fresh buds, but stored or cured (dried) buds and hashish tend to have higher amounts of CBN because the THC has degraded in the preparation process.

The compound associated with the fragrance of the plant is THCV, or Tetrahydrocannabivarin. Very pungent-smelling cannabis usually contains high amounts of THCV, and it's also found in very potent marijuana originating from Southeast and Central Asia and Africa.

Cannabichromene, or CBC, makes up to 20 per cent of the cannabinoid compound of the cannabis plant.

CROSS POLLINATION

Armed with all this knowledge, home-grown horticulturists have taken to splicing, cross-pollinating and nurturing a vast variety of strains. Many breeders now concentrate on developing varieties in the plant by controlling the growth process. This is done in a variety of ways using lamps and bulbs, ventilation and soil nutrients, hydroponics, rock-wool, salt-free sand, etc.

Growing cannabis is a relatively simple task. It's a hardy annual plant that survives well in temperate climates and can be grown in or outdoors in basic soil. In fact it thrives so well in the natural climate of the UK that the local council at Glastonbury, home of the legendary rock festival, have stopped cutting down the wild-growing cannabis. However, to really get the best from the seeds, like any gardening, "It takes years to get really good at it. There are unbelievable amounts of information to learn," one Canadian grower warned.

SEED SELECTION

Cannabis seed selection can be like choosing a fine wine. Plants may be picked for their citrus aromas, or their blueberry taste, for example. It can be mind-boggling for the beginner. There are over 250 branded seed strains available, with at least another 300 unbranded. Potentially the list is endless, as growers experiment with cross-breeding.

With so many new breeders and seed companies coming into the market in recent years, cannabis seeds are a minefield of discussion these days. It's possible to buy seeds on the Internet from top cannabis breeders but the best tend to come from Dutch companies, such as Ben Dronkers' Sensi Seed Bank, and Serious Seeds. Many have a high germination success rate, as they are kept in cannabis-seed storage units which keep them fresh and prevent them from drying out.

The safest and most reliable seeds are top-quality F1 hybrid strains. These are stabilized seeds that have been selectively inbred over several generations so that the desired traits are guaranteed. This process can take up to four years, using a staggering 20,000 plants, but the end result is always worth it. However, there are still companies that sell unstabilized strains (hybrids from hybrids), which have unpredictable results.

Feminized seeds

A relatively new development in seed technology is "feminized seeds." These are seeds that are allegedly guaranteed only to sprout female flowers, avoiding the necessity of having to weed out the male plants in a crop. To feminize seeds, female clones are selected. Under standard conditions these clones do not produce any male flowers, but various methods can make the clones produce abundant male flowers and pollen. The pollen produced by these hermaphrodite herbs is then used to produce feminized seeds.

In 1999, feminized seed pioneers the Dutch Passion Seed Company experimented with 15 varieties of feminized seeds. They started with 30 seeds per variety, with the aim to determine the percentages of female, male and hermaphroditic plants and to compare the uniformity among plants from feminized seeds with those grown

Above (left to right): Cannabis comes in many shapes and colors; the classic Afghan, Double Dutch, and Blueberry.

from "regular" seeds. They discovered that certain environmental factors in the first 2–3 weeks of growth, such as higher nitrogen concentration, higher humidity, lower temperatures and more blue light with fewer "daylight" hours, gave more female plants, whereas a higher potassium concentration gave more males.

While many seed retailers now stock the higher-priced feminized seeds, they remain highly controversial and have split grass growers down the middle, with the opposing camp claiming that they are not 100 per cent guaranteed, and that the process goes against nature.

This is what all first-time growers should aspire to. By following the advice contained in these pages you too can produce top-quality plants.

2

PLANNING YOUR INDOOR GARDEN

PLANNING YOUR INDOOR GARDEN

Harvey Mackay famously said, "Failures don't plan to fail; they fail to plan."

The successful outcome of an outdoor grow will depend on Mother Nature; you will have very little impact on the results, you can labor for months and nature can destroy all your hard work in a matter of hours.

Within an indoor operation the environment is totally controllable and can be balanced to ensure that all the requirements of the plant are met.

What you will need

The most basic requirements are:

- Light
- Heat
- Ventilation
- Food
- Water

To fulfill the above requirements the grow area will require access to water and electricity.

Above: Grow rooms are very hot locations due to the number of high wattage lights in use. Circulation fans ensure this heat is evenly distributed.

Above: A 4 inch (10cm) carbon filter inline extraction fan for removing the odor from the grow room. This will not be required in a very small set-up.

Below: A High Intensity Discharge (H.I.D) lighting ballast, which converts the electricity to the correct voltage for the lamp.

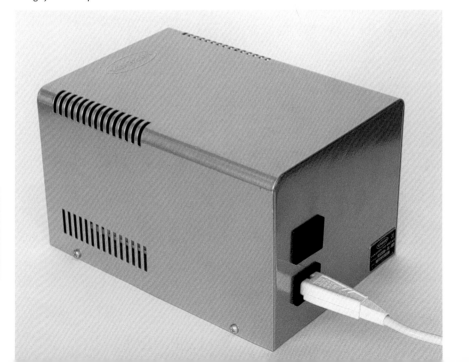

> ### Top Tip
>
> When you have completed reading this book, return to this chapter and then start your plan.

Above: pH and nutrient level testing kits.
For your crop to grow, the medium they are planted in must be pH neutral.

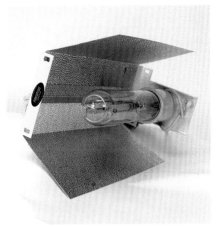

Above: A High Pressure Sodium Lamp, which should be used during the flowering stage.

Above: Gardening pots come in all shapes and sizes. When potting ensure your plants have plenty of room to grow.

Above: An example of a reservoir and tank, typical of a hydroponic set-up.

Above: Like all plants, cannabis will grow more effectively when given food and nutrients. There is a wide selection of plant foods on the market.

Above right: Rockwool is a popular medium for hydroponic gardeners.

Right: Aeroponic propagators are becoming very popular. Aeroponics involves growing without a medium and supplying nutrients via a light misting or fine spray.

Where?

For me the ideal location for an indoor cannabis garden is a basement or cellar; the temperatures in subterranean grow rooms do not suffer the seasonal fluctuations that plague the attic grower. If you are not lucky enough to have access to a basement then you can consider an attic or a spare bedroom; if you cannot spare a whole room for your new hobby then you can convert a closet into a grow chamber.

Wherever you decide to construct your growing area, it should be easily accessible and there should be enough space within the area to move around.

Electricity supply is an essential requirement and if there is not a plentiful supply of wall sockets they will have to be installed. Ensure electrical sockets are situated at least 1 foot (30cm) above the floor. A grow room can be a dangerous place so ensure that any accidental water spills are kept well away from all electrical equipment. NEVER allow electrical equipment to sit on the floor of your grow area.

A good ventilation system will require at least one and possibly two inline extraction fans. Look for locations where there is easy access to a source of fresh air to enter and an exit for stale air to be extracted.

Right: Although basements are preferable, attics and spare rooms are ideal places for setting up your indoor garden.

Safety First

A separate fuse-box or circuit breaker should be used to isolate the whole grow room in the event of a short circuit or similar problem. If you are not a competent electrician get professional help. Cannabis does not kill but electricity can. Be safe!

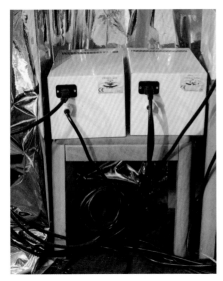

Above: Ensure ballasts and other items of electrical equipment are raised above the floor to avoid contact with water spills.

Above: This closet grow set-up demonstrates what can be achieved with the most modest of space. We explain how you can convert an old closet into a grow room on page 28.

A water supply in or adjacent to your grow room is not essential but it would make life considerably easier.

If you are considering growing in an attic space, bear in mind that these areas tend to suffer from extremes of heat in the summer months. If you are planning to utilize an attic area you must factor in the possibility of installing an air-conditioning unit or accept the possibility of being forced to shut down the room during the summer months.

Having decided upon the location for your indoor garden, you now need to construct a light-proof growing area before starting to cultivate.

Walls should be covered with a reflective surface, not only to direct all light back toward your plants to maximize growth, but also to ensure no light escapes which could otherwise arouse suspicion.

How?

If your chosen area is much larger than you need, build a smaller grow area by partitioning off a section. This will ensure the light is concentrated and a smaller area is also easier to vent and control humidity levels.

If it is not practical to build a permanent structure, a viable option is to purchase a purpose-built grow tent.

If you have the luxury of additional space consider constructing and utilizing separate areas within your grow area for different growth stages:

• A room for vegetative growth or "vegging" can contain mother plants,

clones, seedlings, and of course plants in their vegetative period of growth. The lights in this room should operate 18 or 24 hours per day.

• A separate flowering room is an added expense due to the extra equipment required but if used for a Sea of Green (SOG) (see page 70) operation it can be very productive. The lights in this room would operate on a 12/12 basis i.e. 12 hours on and 12 hours off.

Once you have decided on or constructed your area you need to prepare it.

The room should be enclosed, and everything unrelated to the garden should be removed, as furniture and curtains can harbor fungi and moulds. Fitting a set of blinds (closed) and affixing a stout board to the interior of the window frame is a better option. For a professional job, paint the board matt black.

Lining the walls of the grow area with a reflective surface will help to reflect valuable light back toward your plants and the lining will also assist to create a light-proof growing area.

You can simply paint the interior of your grow area with white paint. However, white paint reflects only 75 per cent of light directed at it. More efficient reflective surfaces can be purchased from good cultivation stores. They will stock a useful plastic material called black and white (B&W)—as the name suggests, it is black on one side and white on the

other and is available on rolls of differing widths. Black and white is 85 per cent reflective and is also easy to fit using a staple gun or the double-sided sticky tape used in fitting carpets.

Another wall-lining material worth consideration is Mylar, a thin plastic sheeting developed by NASA which has an aluminum surface that is 90 per cent reflective. However, the surface will quickly tarnish if it comes into contact with water or chemicals.

Test for light seepage into the grow room by closing yourself inside. Allow enough time for your eyes to adjust to the darkness, the room should be completely dark.

When you are satisfied that the walls are covered and that the room is light proof you can turn your attention to the floor.

Floors should be sealed with a heavy duty plastic which is waterproof, this will make the mopping up of accidental spills easy. Allow for at least a 6 inch (15cm) "overlap" up the wall of the room to ensure a good seal. Damp-proof membranes used by builders are ideal.

Top Tip

If the noise of pumps and fans is likely to be an issue, use polystyrene tiles or similar as sound insulation.

LIGHTS

Lighting specifics are detailed in later chapters, but within your grow area you will need to work out where the lights should be situated. Bear in mind that the height of the lamp needs to be adjustable and this can be achieved by suspending the reflector from the ceiling using lightweight chains fixed to hooks securely attached to a roof truss or beam.

There are various lighting options available but for the beginner either High Intensity Discharge (H.I.D.) lamps, or cultivation Envirolites are the best options.

H.I.D. lighting is the type of lighting used in street lighting; it consists of a reflector, a lamp (bulb), and a ballast. The most common sizes are 250 Watt, 400 Watt, 600 Watt and 1,000 Watt.

A 600 Watt light is a good choice for the beginner and will adequately illuminate an area of three square feet (one square meter).

Above: During the vegetative stage lights will remain on 24 hours a day.

Left: Lights can be heavy, so with larger grow rooms ensure their weight is well supported.

Right: When reflectors are suspended on chains their height is easily adjusted. This is not only essential for adjusting the light and heat available to plants at different stages of the flowering cycle, but also useful for moving the lights out of the way when tending to the plants.

Reflector

The reflector is also known as a canopy or hood and is required to direct or reflect the light downward toward the plant. A lamp or bulb holder is incorporated into the reflector and connected to a ballast via an electrical cable.

Ballast

A ballast is usually a heavy metal boxed unit containing a capacitor, a transformer, and an igniter. These units create a lot of heat, which may be an advantage in a cool room or a distinct disadvantage in a room prone to overheating. Locating the ballast unit inside or outside the room will depend on other factors and the ballast can always be relocated at a later stage if required. However, if you are working in a restricted area where space is at a premium then locate the ballast outside the room.

Ballasts must be attached securely to a wall or sited on a small shelf or raised platform. On no account allow a ballast to sit directly on the floor, where it could come into contact with spilt liquids.

Lamp

There are different types of H.I.D. lamps available. They all use the industry standard E40 fitting and are therefore interchangeable.

Metal Halide emits light in the blue spectrum which is suitable for vegetative growth.

High Pressure Sodium lamps emit light in the red spectrum suitable for flowering and a new lamp should emit 120 lumens per watt.

Agro or Planta lamps are specifically designed to encompass both the red and white spectrum. However, using a Metal Halide for the vegetative stage and a High Pressure Sodium for the flowering period gives the best overall results.

Lamp	Size	Lumens
Sodium	400w	53,000
Sodium	600w	92,000

CONTACTORS AND TIMERS

A timer is a practical and easy way to switch the H.I.D. lights on and off. However, if you connect the lights directly to the timer it will not be able to handle the large surge of current involved in starting up the light. After days or weeks the contacts inside the timer will become "welded" to each other and the timer will not switch off.

Contactors are designed to take the initial load and a quality contactor will ensure your lights operate correctly.

Too much light in a grow room is never a problem. However, too much heat can be a major problem and as H.I.D. lights generate large amounts of heat this has to be controlled.

A fan controller and thermometer and hygrometer.

VENTILATION

Ventilation serves three main purposes: it refreshes stale air, controls humidity, and removes excess heat.

An extractor fan used in a bathroom or kitchen may suffice for a small closet grow but is not recommended for a larger area. They are not designed to run for long periods and wear out quickly.

Inline fans are designed to operate for long periods and are much more efficient at shifting large volumes of air.

Fans come in various sizes:
- A 4 inch (10cm) diameter fan will extract approximately 575 feet (175m) per hour.
- A 5 inch (12cm) diameter fan will extract approximately 740 feet (225m) per hour.
- A 6 inch (15cm) diameter fan will extract approximately 1,380 feet (420m) per hour.

The air in your room should be changed every three minutes—20 times an hour. To calculate the cubic capacity (how big it is) of your room, multiply width x length x height and multiply the answer by 20.

A room measures 6 feet wide, 9 feet long and 6 feet high (1.8 x 2.7 x 1.8m). Multiply the three dimensions together, 6 x 9 x 6 = 324. The cubic capacity of the room is 324 feet and this amount of air will need to be changed 20 times an hour. 324 x 20 = 6,480 feet per hour.

A carbon filter reduces a fan's capacity by approximately 25 per cent so a 5 inch

An air extraction system is essential for larger grow rooms where the aroma is strong.

(12cm) would really struggle; a far better option would be to use a 6 inch (15cm) fan. An advantage of a larger fan is that you can operate it at lower speeds, which will reduce noise levels.

Having constructed and sealed your light-proof grow area you now need to cut a suitable hole to take the exhaust ducting for the fan.

Fixing the fan to a wall or ceiling can result in some vibration noise, especially if the fan is working at full speed. Suspending the fan with bungee type cords will reduce vibration significantly.

When your fan is secured, connect ducting to the fan outlet (there are usually arrows marked on the fan casing showing the direction of air flow), run the ducting through the hole you have just cut, and seal any gaps between the ducting and the side of the hole.

Connect another length of ducting to the fan inlet and attach the other end to your carbon filter. Since hot air rises it is more efficient to site the filter at the

apex of the grow space or at least level with the light.

You now need to consider how and where fresh air is going to enter your grow area. Passive air intakes cut into the bottom of the grow chamber will allow air to be drawn inside. The intakes will need to be light-proofed; this is easily achieved by constructing a simple baffle out of cardboard.

An additional inline fan can be used to draw fresh air into your room instead of the passive inlets.

Top Tip

A 5 inch (12cm) fan running at 70 per cent capacity is quieter and will last a lot longer than a 4 inch (10cm) fan operating at maximum capacity.

TEMPERATURE

Cannabis plants will thrive between 68°F (20°C) and 82°F (28°C), temperatures in excess of 86°F (30°C) should be avoided. Air conditioning units can be used to control the temperature. However, the best method is to extract the hot, humid, stale air and replace it with clean, drier, cooler air.

STALE AIR

Carbon dioxide (CO_2) is essential to plant growth and a cannabis plant will rapidly consume all the available Co_2 within a grow room. When this happens, plants just stop growing.

Leaving the door open on a small closet or cabinet grow is not as efficient or productive as a proper ventilation system. However, if you are on a limited budget it is an option.

Top Tip

Mopping up all spills, covering nutrient tanks, and covering the rooting medium will reduce the evaporation process and therefore the humidity.

HUMIDITY

Relative humidity is measured as a percentage, it is a measure of the amount of water vapor in the air and is linked to temperature. In your indoor garden for every 68°F (20°C) increase in temperature the humidity will double.

During the vegetative stage the ideal humidity level is around 50 per cent; during the later stages of flowering the humidity levels should be reduced to avoid the risk of bud rot developing.

Plants transpire and this process will raise the humidity level in your room; if the humidity reaches 70 per cent or higher there is a danger of gray mold (Botrytis) developing. This horrible fungus has destroyed more cannabis crops than the DEA. It produces a gray fungal growth and the early signs are a discoloration and/or a wilting of the leaves.

To decrease the humidity levels, simply increase the air exchange rate, i.e. get your fans working more often and for longer periods. If the humidity is really high leave the fan running continuously during the period when the lights are on.

THERMOMETER AND HYGROMETER

This useful device measures and displays temperature and relative humidity. Try to obtain one with a maximum/minimum memory as this enables you to see the extremes for both temperature and humidity within your grow room.

FAN CONTROL

A variable speed controller does just that, it allows you to set the speed of the fan giving you more control—e.g. increase the fan speed to reduce humidity and temperature.

An automatic fan controller will allow you to set the humidity and temperature range limits. For the vegetative stage set the humidity control to 50 per cent and the temperature to 86°F (30°C). When the levels rise above your set limits the fan will be activated and will deactivate when the temperature and the humidity have fallen below your set parameters.

Top Tip

If you are on a tight budget, use a conventional timer to control the on/off of the fan. Set the fan to come on and off during the light cycle only.

FILTERS

Cannabis is a very pungent plant with a very distinctive odor. Venting directly from your flowering room is a serious security risk and a sure way of inviting unwanted attention.

The easiest way to resolve this serious problem is to attach a carbon filter to the extraction fan. The filter is secured within the grow room and connected to the inline extraction fan. When the fan is operated air is drawn from the room, through the filter, and smell particles are absorbed by the activated charcoal particles in the filter.

Replace the filters every 12 to 18 months.

CIRCULATION

The circulation of the air within your grow room is also an essential requirement and is achieved by using oscillating fans.

When a plant takes up water, it transpires—that is, it exhales water vapor through pores located on the underside of the leaves called stomata. If the air is not moving, stratification takes place, the dead air underneath the leaves reduces or stops the stomata from feeding and growth is restricted.

Another advantage of using an oscillating fan is the effect it has on the stems and branches—the constant swaying to and fro strengthens the plants, which will help them to support the weight of the big fat buds that are hopefully going to develop.

Plants benefit from the movement of air generated by circulation fans—the constant swaying to and fro helps strengthen the branches.

Top Tip

An oscillating fan directed toward the light will cool the lamp and allow the light to be brought closer to the plants. This will increase yields!

Building a Growdrobe

An old closet can easily be converted into a cultivation chamber using the same principles applicable in the construction of a grow room.

Most closets will benefit from some additional structural support: a 1/2 inch (1cm) thick plywood sheet screwed to the rear of the closet will usually suffice.

1 Cut a 4 inch (10cm) diameter hole in the rear of the closet approximately 6 inch (15cm) from the top. This will allow for extraction.

2 Drill six, 2 inch (5cm) air "intake" holes in a horizontal line along the rear of the closet approx. 12 inches (30cm) from the floor.

3 Line the interior walls of the chamber with reflective material (Mylar).

4 Secure a 4 inch (10cm) inline extractor fan to the "ceiling" of the chamber. If you are on a budget you can use a bathroom type extractor and if so then it is a good idea to place a sheet of polystyrene between the fan and the side of the closet to limit any noise caused through vibration.

Top Tip

If you wish to maximize the space in your Growdrobe, situate the inline fan and the lighting ballast outside.

Use a desk-type circulation fan to provide air movement within the Growdrobe.

Top Tip

Before introducing plants into your grow area clean all surfaces with a disinfectant or a 5 per cent bleach solution (5 per cent bleach and 95 per cent water, by volume). This will help to avoid the development of pests and bacteria.

An H.I.D. light in the small confined space of a closet will require a lot of ventilation to remove any excess heat, and in such a small space even a 250w light will produce a lot of warmth. A good alternative is to use Envirolites, blue for vegetative growth and red spectrum for flowering. These lights produce little heat and can therefore be placed very close to the plants.

Above: A disused closet, such as this, makes a great Growdrobe with some fairly minor modifications.

ORGANIC OR HYDRO?

So, having constructed your full-on grow room, closet, or Growdrobe, installed ventilation, filtration, light, circulation, and control equipment, how are you going to cultivate?

The basic choice is hydroponics or organic. There is no right or wrong choice to be made here, it depends on your personal preferences. In fact, many growers start out with one method and change to another and then back again.

I first started out by growing organically and since then have used both organic and hydro methods.

In my opinion, beginners will generally find using traditional pots with soil the easiest option. Soil is a pH buffer and can therefore be more forgiving than hydroponic systems, which generally are more complicated.

Left: An organic grow room, proper gardening! In my opinion first-time growers will find cannabis cultivation easier using pots and soil, at least to begin with.

WHICH VARIETY?

There is a bewildering variety of cannabis plants available, over 1,400, and that figure is increasing week by week as breeders create new strains.

A good choice for first-time growers would be a well-established strain with stable genetics, ideally an indica variety because they are short, bushy, and easy to grow.

Above: When choosing your strain, be sure to pick something that is well-established and comparatively easy to grow.

3

PLANNING YOUR OUTDOOR GARDEN

PREPARING THE SOIL

If you are going to grow outdoors, it is best to start early. Ideally the preparation of your soil should begin in the Fall prior to planting.

Firstly, give the earth a good dig over, check for and remove any large root systems (minor roots can be severed or removed) and remove large stones.

Establish the soil pH with a pH testing kit or pH soil meter (readily available from garden centers). Soil pH should be between pH 6.0 and pH 7.0—to raise the pH add garden lime and to lower add ground sulfur.

To ensure your young plants get off to a good start it is essential that the soil is treated with a feed rich in nitrogen. Fish, blood, bone meal, or a slow-release fertilizer should be added evenly over the entire grow area and worked well into the soil.

What strains are best for outdoor?

Your choice of strain will be dependent on your location—a 20 foot (6m) Sativa plant is ideal if you have a spacious garden but is impractical if you are confined to a small backyard. If space is an inhibiting factor then opt for the shorter cannabis Indica varieties, but be aware that some Indica varieties can grow to 7 or 8 feet (2.5m).

Early flowering cannabis varieties that

Above: When choosing an outdoor spot to plant in bear in mind that your plants should blend in with the surrounding environment.

are mold- and disease-resistant which finish around mid-September are a good choice for outdoor cultivation. Long-flowering varieties are prone to attacks from bud-rot due to the damp conditions experienced in the Fall.

When to plant outdoors

This depends on the growing season in your part of the world. However, it should be after the last frost of the Spring. For most of us in the Western world that will be after April/May.

You can start your plants off indoors from as early as late March. Calculate how many plants you will require and use

Above: Planting clones guarantees that the mature plants will be female.

Below: Tools essential for the outdoor gardener.

clones or seeds as detailed in Chapter 5. Bear in mind that if you are starting from seed you will need to germinate twice as many seeds as the number of plants you require, to allow for the loss of the male plants.

After a couple of weeks, when the young plants have been re-potted, you can gradually acclimatize the plants by moving them outdoors during the day.

Final planting out either directly into prepared ground or into larger containers should take place around mid-May.

WHAT FOOD?

Cannabis plants in their vegetative growth stage require feeds rich in nitrogen such as Bio-Bizz Fish Mix or a fertilizer with an NPK of 30-15-15. The NPK ratio denotes:

N = Nitrogen

P = Phosphorus

K = Potassium

When the flowering stage commences the plant will require lower levels of nitrogen and higher levels of phosphorus, which promotes bud growth. Fertilizers

with an NPK of 15-30-30 are perfect.

Young plants will benefit from additives such as seaweed extract, which contains growth hormones and will promote the creation of healthy roots.

Further information on feeding plants will be found in later chapters.

PESTS

Larger pests like rabbits can be deterred by erecting a small fence made from wire mesh; make sure it is pinned to the ground to avoid predators pushing under the wire. Camouflage with grass and bracken if possible.

Below: Fencing in your plot can help eliminate pests.

Smaller but no less damaging pests can be controlled by the application of an organic pesticide, but ensure it is suitable for food use.

> **Top Tip**
>
> Some outdoor growers urinate around their plants in the belief that their scent will deter animals from the area.

> **Top Tip**
>
> Neem oil is a 100 per cent organic natural insect repellent suitable for outdoor use.

Your plant is unlikely ever to reach this size, but it might still benefit from some training.

TRAINING

Most plants will require some sort of training or support. If your plant is growing faster and higher than you anticipated, there are a couple of things you can do to make it more manageable. Very tall plants can be bent downward and tied down with twine secured to pegs hammered into the ground.

Large bushy plants can be held down with wide-meshed plastic netting and again secured with pegs hammered into the ground. You will find that branches and buds will grow up through the netting and the plant will continue to grow as normal.

Top Tip

It is possible to force flower at any time of the year by moving the plants indoors into a light-proof shed or garage (if small enough). Place inside at 7 p.m. and take outside the next day at 7 a.m.

A very productive method of cannabis cultivation is called Screen of Green, also known as SCROG. This method requires an area of wide-meshed netting to be secured approx. 18 to 24 inches (45–60cm) above and parallel to the plant or plants.

As the plants' stems grow through the mesh they are gently bent downward and "weaved" in and out of the mesh. The intention is to create a screen of buds; all the foliage beneath the screen is removed to leave the bare stems.

SCROG is suitable for organic and hydroponic cultivation.

FLOWERING OUTDOORS

Flowering commences when the plant receives 12 hours of total darkness. Outdoor flowering will naturally occur as the day length decreases. This varies depending where in the world you live.

GREENHOUSE

For large greenhouses it is preferable to plant directly into the soil, but for the average greenhouse growing in containers is a more practical option. To control the temperature fix a thermostatically operated automatic window closer.

The amount of control over the interior environment will be greatly increased if electric power can be provided to the greenhouse. The addition of an electric supply will allow for the use of extraction and circulation fans, and there is also the possibility of using an ozone generator to deter pests and eliminate any odor.

Supplementary lighting can be used within a greenhouse, but only in extremely remote locations.

An outdoor grow can produce fantastic results.

POTS AND PATIOS

Growers use a wide range of pots: small, large, round, square, tall, and short. Cannabis plants have a long root structure and therefore a tall, deep pot or container is the ideal choice.

Square pots can be used to get plants closer together to make the maximum use of the available space.

As the plants grow they will require re-potting as described in Chapter 5. Suggested pot sizes:

- 3 inch for seedlings and cuttings
- 4 inch for young (unsexed) plants
- 8 inch and larger for final potting
- 4 gallon containers give enough space for a healthy root system to develop and yet remain moveable.

OUTDOOR LOCATIONS

The main factor in ensuring a successful garden is the location. Woodland, scrubland, and even waste ground can be used. A good location will have a plentiful supply of water and be south-facing. The soil should also be well drained, not boggy, and prepared as described at the beginning of this section. The site should also receive direct sunlight for at least five or six hours per day.

The minimum number of journeys to an outdoor location would be:

- To prepare the site
- Once to plant and feed
- Two more visits to administer feeds
- Last feed around mid-August
- Final visit to the site to harvest the crop

The above regime is based upon approximately six weeks between feeds, no watering and an average eight-week flowering requirement.

An outdoor site does not have to be very large; a clearing measuring 6 feet x 6 feet (1.8 x 1.8m) can accommodate five large plants if they are arranged in an "X" shape. Ensure there is enough cover around the site to protect your plants.

Of course, planting your site can be as simple as sowing seeds directly into the ground. The disadvantage with this method is that you will have to return at a later date to remove the males. If you get the timing of your visit wrong there is also the added risk of the male plants pollinating the females.

If you absolutely have to use seeds, then consider germinating and sexing them at home and then transport the female seedlings to the site for planting. Using clones is by far the easiest option.

Cannabis plants offer an attractive variation when placed alongside more traditional patio plants.

Left: Removing weeds and other plants from the vicinity ensures the cannabis plant receives the maximum amount of light.

Below: With an outdoor grow, confine harvesting to the main stems and side shoots.

OUTDOOR HARVESTING

The optimum time of day to crop an outdoor grow is supposedly first thing in the morning. However, I prefer to crop later in the day when the morning dew has evaporated away.

Outdoor harvesting should be confined to main stems and side shoots with heavy buds. You can leave the majority of the plant, it may regenerate.

How to dry and cure your harvest is covered in Chapter 8.

HYDROPONICS

SIMPLY HYDROPONIC

Hydroponics quite simply means growing without soil, using a liquid solution which contains all the nutrients and minerals required to produce a healthy plant.

Many experienced growers prefer hydroponic cultivation due to the faster growth rates and impressive yields. This method of cultivation is certainly within the capabilities of the novice grower. However, beginners need to be aware that hydroponic cultivation can be extremely unforgiving and mistakes can be punished to excess.

Hydroponic systems can be classified as either Active Hydroponics, where the nutrient solution is pumped from a nutrient tank, or Passive Hydroponics, where the nutrient solution is delivered to the plants by non-mechanical means.

There are relative benefits to each type of hydroponic growing. However, in each instance a tank should be made up containing the nutrient solution that needs to be fed to the plants, and the solution will need to be monitored and adjusted in a similar manner.

Given the amount of water use and the presence of electrical appliances, safety is an even more important consideration than with organic growing. It is also advised to tape the plastic floor coverings thoroughly to avoid mess as a result of spillages.

Above: Given the amount of water involved in hydroponic growing, it is recommended that you cover the flooring with plastic sheeting so it is protected in the event of any spillages.

Right: A standard hydro set-up in an attic.

The Wick System

Passive hydroponics is the cheapest and simplest method of hydroponic growing available and the simplest method is the wick system.

This basic system uses the principle of capillary action. The plant is fed via lengths of $\frac{1}{2}$ inch (1cm) diameter, braided nylon rope, which are used as wicks to draw a nutrient solution from a reservoir to the plant.

Plants are grown in conventional pots or containers and the wicks run from the medium through small, tight-fitting holes into the nutrient solution contained in the reservoir.

Increasing the number or length of the wicks or their thickness will increase the amount of nutrient solution delivered to the medium.

A medium-mix containing a combination of vermiculite, perlite, and clay pebbles is a good medium for this system. The bottom inch of the container should be filled with vermiculite only. As vermiculite is very absorbent the wicks will then have an optimum medium for moisture transfer.

ACTIVE HYDROPONIC SYSTEMS

Active systems use an electric pump and vary from a simple homemade bubbler bucket to specialist aeroponic grow chambers. One of the more popular systems is:

NFT (Nutrient Film Technique)

NFT is a very simple system. A nutrient solution is pumped from a reservoir to the top of an inclined tray. The solution then flows down the length of the tray, feeding and watering the plants as it goes (pictured right).

To ensure the even distribution of the nutrient solution, the base of the inclined tray is covered by capillary matting called a spreader mat. Always allow the spreader mat to overhang the lower end of the tray; this provides an easy return path for the nutrient solution to the reservoir.

The nutrient solution returns to the reservoir under gravity and is re-circulated by a submersible electric pump running 24/7.

The addition of a corrugated plastic top plate will stop light reaching the nutrient solution and complete darkness prevents algae growth.

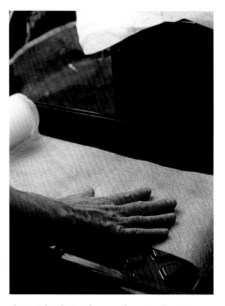

Above: When laying the spreader mat, allow it to overhang the lower end of the tray so it can reach the nutrient solution in the reservoir.

Above: Cut holes in the corrugated plastic top plate to make room for the plants.

Planting in NFT

The leading medium for use in NFT systems is Rockwool cubes.

Large Rockwool cubes have a hole in the top which accepts a smaller Rockwool propagation cube.

When your seedlings or clones have developed strong healthy white roots to the outside of the small propagation plug, they can be transplanted into a Rockwool cube.

Rockwool cubes should be pre-soaked overnight in pH-adjusted water (5.5 to 6.2). Gently squeeze the block prior to use, the cube should be damp and not waterlogged.

Hand-feed the young plants in the cubes with a half strength hydroponic nutrient solution. Plants will be ready to transplant to your NFT system when

Below: The plastic cover will ensure that the plant's root system is protected from light.

Above: A typical NFT tray used in hydroponic gardening.

there is an abundance of white healthy roots protruding from the Rockwool cube.

Under the correct conditions root growth is amazingly rapid and it is not unusual to see several inches of new root growth daily.

Top Tip

Maintain the temperature of your nutrient solution between 64–71°F (18–22°C), by placing a thermostatically controlled aquarium heater in the reservoir.

ROOTS

As with all forms of gardening, the secret of success is to establish a productive, healthy root system and with NFT it is essential to have a healthy root system bursting from the medium.

A healthy plant root system consists of three main components:

Primary roots—are the large-diameter roots which first emerge from the propagation block into the nutrient solution.

Secondary roots—emerge from the primary roots. The large surface area of these roots makes them vital in taking up nutrients and water from the nutrient solution.

Root hairs—take up oxygen from the atmosphere. It is essential to keep the flowing solution from pooling in the tray, otherwise these hairs become submerged in the solution and cannot access oxygen in the atmosphere.

Above: Roots should be abundant, white, and healthy. This specimen is about to be transplanted into an AutoPot containing coir.

Left: You can check if a plant requires feeding by "weighing" the pot in your hands.

Ebb and Flood

Also known as flood and drain. This system is generally used with clay pebbles in a container that sits on top of a reservoir. A pump connected to a timer pumps the nutrient solution until the container is full; this is known as the flood cycle. The nutrient drains slowly back into the reservoir through small drain holes; this is the ebb or drain cycle. As the solution drains away, air is drawn down into the medium and this action provides fresh oxygen to the root system.

The cycle usually occurs two to three times during the light period. Environmental factors, the type of medium being used, and the growth stage of the plant will dictate how many complete feeding cycles are required.

AutoPots

The AutoPot system is essentially a passive hydroponic set-up that can be used with a whole range of mediums.

Controlling the system is a simple mechanical device, which is best described as a "vacuum float valve." This Smart Valve™ is gravity fed via a reservoir or water butt—the system does not require electricity, pumps, or timers and is easy to extend. When the plant has used all the nutrient solution in the AutoPot, the valve will open allowing the pot to refill. The unique factor of this system is that it is actually controlled by the plant!

The single 3.5 gallon (15 liter) pot unit has a side compartment which contains the SmartValve™. This system is very versatile and easily extended.

Above: AutoPots are linked to one another by tubing, so all plants are fed by the same water/nutrient supply.

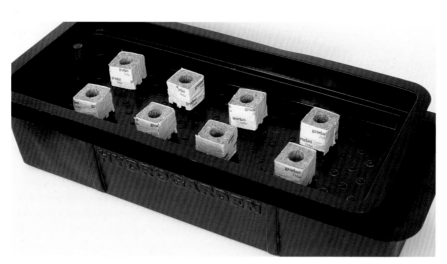

Above: The ebb and flood system. Water automatically fills the top tray and drains back into the reservoir through the tiny holes shown.

Right: The SmartValve™ system in the AutoPot allows the plant to dictate when it is fed and watered.

A young White Rhino plant in coir. Coir, or coconut fiber, is totally organic and has an excellent air-to-moisture ratio.

Mediums

The choice of potting medium which can be used with the AutoPot systems is both wide and varied; the choice of medium for many growers will be what suits their personal preference. Successful mediums have very good capillary action, good air-to-moisture ratio, and are pH stable.

Many different mediums have been used successfully in these systems, including soil, coir (coconut fiber), perlite, vermiculite, Rockwool, and combinations of them all.

For me, coir is by far the best performing medium and has many advantages over its alternatives. Coir is totally organic, which means it will compost well after use, and if disposed of in your backyard it will help to improve your soil quality. Coir also has excellent air-to-moisture ratio.

Top Tip

Large tanks should be kept agitated to prevent nutrients settling at the bottom. Use an air stone connected to an air pump or a small hydroponic nutrient pump.

NUTRIENTS

Plants require around 20 basic elements to ensure healthy growth. The three most commonly known are nitrogen, phosphorus and potassium—abbreviated to NPK. The remaining elements are called Micro-Elements and whereas these elements are present in soil, they have to be added to hydroponic nutrient solution.

Hydroponic stores stock a bewildering choice of nutrient solutions. There are two-part solutions, which have to be mixed together in set amounts of water, and even three-part solutions. All solutions are also available in soft or hard water options.

If you are unsure about using multi-part solutions, opt for an easier-to-use one-part nutrient.

As with cannabis plants grown organically, hydroponic nutrients fulfill the requirements of the plant for the vegetative and flowering stages. Beginners to hydroponics should keep things simple—you will only require three nutrient solutions for successful cultivation:

- A growth nutrient
- A flowering nutrient
- A flower boost, which aids bud production

How to measure the strength of the nutrient solution

The nutrients and salts contained in the nutrient solution conduct small amounts of electricity, which can be measured by passing a tiny electrical current through the solution. The more dissolved solids contained in a solution the stronger it is.

Conductivity meters

There are many types of conductivity meter (CF) on the market. Personally I use the Bluelab Truncheon.®

It has an easy-to-read, illuminated display and it never requires calibrating.

The conductivity level of the nutrient solution measures the strength of the solution.

A CF or EC meter ensures that optimum nutrient levels are maintained. It is important that your plants are given the correct nutrients—they need about 20 basic elements in all.

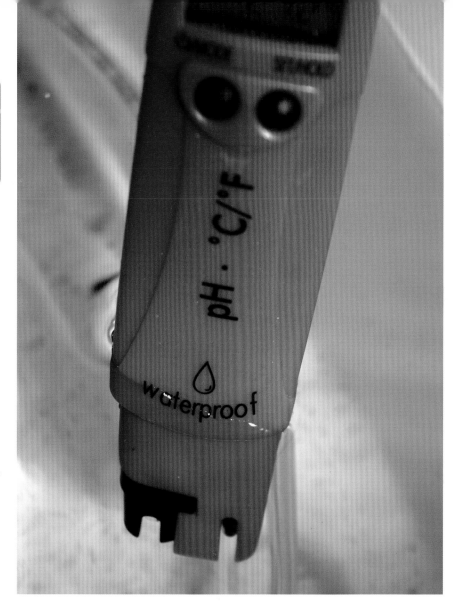

A pH pen is more convenient to use than the chemical test kits. For your plants to grow healthily they need to be in a pH neutral (5.8 to 6.5) medium.

Top Tip

Systems using a reservoir should have the nutrient solution changed at least once every two weeks.

pH

Check the pH level after checking and adjusting the nutrient level.

pH is simply the measure of the acid content of a solution. The pH scale runs from 1 to 14—1 being very acidic, 7 is neutral, and 14 is very alkaline.

pH affects the ability of a plant to absorb nutrients; the optimum range for nutrient absorption is 5.8 to 6.5.

pH can be measured with a cheap chemical test kit or a digital pH meter. Most meters are of the "pen" type. To take a pH reading, simply place your pH meter into the nutrient solution. The LCD display will flash while the measurement is being calculated. When the display stabilizes, the pH level of the solution will be displayed.

Rinse the probe after use in fresh water and replace the storage cap. Clean and calibrate regularly to ensure the pH truncheon remains accurate.

To lower the pH, add phosphoric acid. To raise the pH level, add an alkaline solution such as potassium hydroxide.

Top Tip

When you add an acid or alkaline solution to adjust the pH of your nutrient solution, use a pipette and add very small amounts at a time.

Build your own system

A very effective deep-water culture (DWC) system can be constructed for a minimal cost from a bucket with a lid, an air pump, an air stone, and some tubing. Although this method of cultivation is simple to operate, it is very hands-on and will require daily attention, which is why I think it is an ideal set-up for beginners.

This simple system is capable of producing very impressive results—yields in double figures are not unheard of.

To make your own DWC system you will need the following items:

- 1 x Air stone
- 1 x 4½ feet (1.4m) of plastic airline
- 1 x Air pump
- 1 x 3 inch (7.5cm) Mesh pot
- Clay pebbles (above available from good aquarium stores)
- 1 x Light-proof bucket with a lid, 1 gallon (20 to 25 liters)

3 Pass the airline through the drill hole.

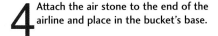

4 Attach the air stone to the end of the airline and place in the bucket's base.

1 Cut a hole in the bucket lid to fit the mesh pot.

2 Drill a ⅕ inch (0.5cm) hole ¾ inch (2cm) below the rim of the bucket, above.

5 Attach the other end of the airline to the air pump.

6 Place the lid onto the top of the bucket and fit the mesh pot into the hole, right.

7 Fill the bucket with water until the water level reaches the base of the mesh pot.

8 Turn the air pump on, and allow the bucket to sit for 24 hours.

Top Tip

It is important to raise the air pump above the level of the bucket, to stop liquid being drawn into the pump. Alternatively, fit a one-way check valve (available from aquarium stores).

A white piece of plastic on top of the bucket lid reflects light upward to the lower buds.

Operating the DWC bucket

Pre-soak the clay pebbles for 24 hours in water with a pH of 5.8 to 6.5.

Place the clone or seedling into the net pot with the clay pebbles and pack pebbles around the rooting medium.

Place the net pot in the hole in the bucket lid.

The air bubbles breaking the surface of the nutrient solution will spray and splash the net pot and, as the root system develops, the nutrient level should be lowered.

When there is a good root ball bursting from the net pot, drop the nutrient level to about halfway down the bucket. The majority of the roots should hang down into the aerated nutrient solution.

The CF and pH in this type of system is in a constant state of flux, so check the readings daily.

Nutrient solutions in this system should not be used at full strength; only use a nutrient solution that has been mixed to a third of the recommended strength.

The finished homemade bubbler bucket situated in a grow tent and containing a young White Rhino plant.

FLUSHING

Cannabis plants grown in hydroponic systems require a minimum flushing period of 48 hours prior to harvest. Flushing is achieved by replacing the flowering nutrient solution in the system reservoir with plain water.

During the final week of the flowering period cannabis plants will stop the uptake of nutrients and will actually start to return nutrients back into the solution. Replacing the nutrient solution with plain water assists with nutrient removal from the plant and the flushing process will encourage healthy growth.

During the flushing period, regularly check the CF level of the water in your reservoir with your conductivity meter. You will notice that the conductivity level will rise as the plant expels nutrients into the water.

In areas with hard water you will need to flush for a week or so. In this instance the water solution in the tank should be replaced with fresh water at least twice.

Top Tip

The DWC bucket system is designed to operate 24/7. Never turn the air pump off.

It is important to clean up thoroughly after every harvest by emptying planting pots of all mediums and washing them.

PROPAGATION

GROWING FROM SEED

The availability of cannabis seeds will depend on the law in your country, so please ensure you are aware of your local laws and statutes. If your part of the world allows for the legal sale and possession of cannabis seeds then your local headshop should stock a wide choice of strains and varieties.

A common mistake for beginners is to choose an expensive hybrid variety, some of which can be very temperamental. I would recommend going for an established, stable, and forgiving strain such as Skunk #1.

A more expensive option is to buy feminized cannabis seeds. These seeds are 99 per cent guaranteed to produce females. However, plants grown from

There are more than 1,400 cannabis strains available so the new grower is spoilt for choice. I would recommend going for an established strain, such as Skunk #1.

Top Tip

If you need to store seeds for a long period, keep them in their original packaging in an airtight container and place in a fridge (not freezer). Under these conditions seeds can be stored for many years without any loss of vigor.

feminized seed can be prone to stressing.

Some seeds, known as "bag seeds," are the result of poor cultivation techniques. Bag seeds are genetically unstable and should only be germinated if there are no viable alternatives.

Remember: Poor-quality seeds will produce poor-quality plants.

Germination

Seed germination can be as simple as placing a seed directly into the moistened growing medium and if this is to be your chosen method you can increase your chances of success by pre-soaking the seeds overnight in a container of pH neutral water.

Seeds contain 20 per cent moisture; when this increases to above 80 per cent the germination process is activated. One of the simplest and most effective germination methods is the saucer method.

Place a few sheets of absorbent paper onto a shallow plate or saucer and dampen with tepid water. The paper should be moist and not soaked.

Then, evenly space the seeds on the moist paper.

To ensure that the seeds do not dry out, cover the plate with a clear plastic bag or cling film and place in a warm (70–86°F/20–30°C) and dark location. An airing closet is an ideal environment for this.

Check the seeds on a daily basis, paying particular attention to the temperature and the moisture content of the tissue paper. If necessary, remoisten the tissue paper and under NO circumstances allow the paper to dry out.

After a couple of days, and usually within 36 to 48 hours, the seed case will split and the white radicle or root will appear. The seed can now be planted into the rooting medium.

Above: Before you handle any seeds, ensure your hands are clean.

Make a small hole approximately ½ inch (1cm) deep in your chosen medium and VERY carefully transplant the seed into the hole. Ensure the root is pointing downward and then gently cover the seed with the medium. During the transplanting process avoid exposing the tender root to prolonged periods of intense light.

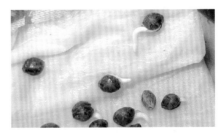

Above: The above seeds have been germinated on dampened tissue; note the radicle emerging from the seed case.

Place seeds approximately ¼ inch (12mm) deep in the planting medium.

Rockwool cubes can be used instead of soil or other mediums.

PROPAGATION

After transplanting into your chosen medium, place the seedlings into a propagator and apply a quarter strength nutrient solution to the medium, ensuring that the medium does not become waterlogged.

Place the propagator under a fluorescent light, low-wattage HID, Envirolite, or on a windowsill. Avoid strong light.

The radicle will continue to develop growing down through the medium and will emerge from the bottom of the medium as a tap root. The stem (hypocotyls) will emerge from the surface of the medium and you will notice two small seed leaves (cotyledons). If the empty seed case is attached to the top of the stem, do not be tempted to remove

it as the seedlings are very delicate and fragile and you may inadvertently damage it in the process.

When there is evidence of a healthy root system emerging from the base of the medium and the first true leaves have developed, the seedling will be ready to transplant or re-pot.

Young plants do not require high levels of light. Fluorescents are ideal for propagation.

SEXING

Growing from seed will produce a male or a female cannabis plant. To determine the sex of a cannabis plant, expose the plant to a 12-hour uninterrupted "dark cycle" per day. After approximately two weeks the plant's sex will be identifiable. In the early stages this can sometimes be difficult to spot with the naked eye so using a magnifying glass will help this process.

Males usually show their sex first and can be identified early by the production of small pollen sacks which resemble a club-shaped (as in playing card type of club) pre-flower.

Females will produce one or two small white hairs, called pistils, which will develop into dense, lovely buds.

Above: The pistil hairs of the female, soon to become buds.

Right: Male pollen sacks. As soon as you have identified any plants as male destroy them to prevent them from pollinating the females.

To avoid your crop being destroyed it is essential you identify the males from females as early as possible. Because it is not always easy to see signs of sexing with the naked eye a jeweler's magnifying glass is a useful tool.

Once the male plants have been identified they must be cut down and disposed of to avoid them contaminating the female plants with pollen.

The female plants can be returned to vegetative growth by changing the light cycle from 12/12 (12 hours of light and 12 hours of darkness per day) to continuous light.

Alternatively, cuttings can be made from un-sexed plants and these can be flowered. Mark plants and cuttings so you can trace them back.

The use of feminized seed or clones will avoid the need for sexing.

Top Tip

Retain a healthy female plant as a Mother plant. She can be used to produce female clones for future crops.

MOTHER PLANTS

A mother plant is a female kept in a permanent vegetative state for the purpose of taking cuttings which will be flowered.

Whether your mother plant is grown from seed or a clone she should be fed with a food with a high nitrogen content. Ensure she is a minimum of eight weeks old before you take any cuttings from her and remember that giving birth is very stressful so always allow the mother sufficient time to recover.

An untended cannabis plant will generally grow to produce a central stem with offshoots. You can encourage the production of side shoots through a process named "pinching out." This is achieved by pinching out the growing tip, slightly above a leaf node.

This process will train the mother plant and provide a good source of cuttings.

A healthy mother is essential to a successful cloning operation.

Top Tip

Look after your mother: never take more than a third of the mother's overall mass, to do so risks stressing her excessively.

These young clones are progressing well, evidenced by white healthy roots emerging from the medium.

Top Tip

• Natural organic honey can be used as a rooting agent.

• Gel or liquid rooting compounds are favored over powdered ones as powders can clog up the stem and stop the cutting breathing as it should.

• If you are using Rockwool propagation plugs, pre-soak them for 24 hours in a container of water with a pH of 5.5. Gently squeeze the plugs to remove excess liquid and use a matchstick or similar to create a suitable hole approx. 1 inch (2.5cm) deep to hold the cutting.

• Add a drop of rooting gel to the hole in the medium.

CLONES

Clones are exact genetic copies of the donor plant.

All parts of the plant can be used for a cutting providing that they have a growing tip, i.e. young green soft stems and shoots. It is easier to take cuttings from the top of the plant but all parts including the lower canopy can and should be used.

Taking cuttings

1 Suitable cuttings will be healthy with at least three sets of leaf nodes and around 3 inches (7–8cm) in length. Identify a suitable branch/shoot and cut with a pair of sharp scissors.

2 Place the shoot onto a clean surface (a chopping board is perfect) and, with a scalpel or razor blade, remove leaves except the two at the top. The cutting needs some leaf to ensure that photo-synthesis can take place. This will produce the energy required to develop a new healthy root system (left and above).

3 Cut the stem at an angle of 45 degrees a fraction below a node (left). (The stem is cut at the 45-degree angle to expose the maximum area.) Dip the cut stem into some fresh tepid water, this will stop an "air bubble" forming in the stem center; alternatively, pop the cutting into your mouth, but NOT if you smoke tobacco as this will contaminate it.

4 Remove the cutting from the water, shake gently to remove excess water and gently "shave" the bottom of the stem from the base to the first node. Holding the scalpel/razor blade parallel to the stem and gently "scraping" the surface of the stem produces the best results (left).

5 Dip the shaved bottom of the cutting into a hormone rooting solution or gel and ensure that the area is well covered (right).

6 Plant the cutting into the hole in the medium and gently pack the medium around the base (below).

7 Place into a propagator and lightly mist the cuttings. Without a root system the cutting will have to rely on "breathing" through its leaves, so misting the cuttings with tepid water will raise the humidity.

After a couple of days, open the vents slightly to replace stale air.

Mist twice daily, and add a weak foliar feed if preferred.

Clones require low light levels, 18 to 24 hours of fluorescents are fine.

An ideal environment for cuttings to thrive in is when the rooting medium is 75 to 80°F (24–26°C) with the air temperature 5 to 10°F lower and a humidity level over 90 per cent.

A heat pad placed under the propagator will encourage good root growth.

After seven days, cuttings should look erect and healthy. Wilted or poorly looking cuttings should be removed.

Between one to three weeks, cuttings should be rooted. Check for signs of roots emerging from the medium.

What to look for:

Day 1—a little wilting is normal.
Day 2—plants should look a little livelier.
Day 3—cuttings should be standing to attention, no signs of wilting.
Day 4—as above, leaves should have a good green healthy color.
Day 7—if yellowing and wilting are evident, then discard cutting after breaking open the medium to examine the root structure.

In the second week, cuttings should have developed enough roots for the clone to take up nutrients and water from its medium. Add a weak (quarter strength) nutrient solution and open vents.

In the third week, roots should be evident on the outside. It is now time to remove the propagator lid.

Below: Keep a close eye on your clones to check for any signs of wilting, etc. Only transplant the clones when a healthy root system is visible through the bottom of the medium.

8 Only transplant when a healthy dense root system is evident.

TRANSPLANTING

Whether grown from seed or cuttings, your young cannabis plant will require transplanting.

1 Place the stem of the young plant in between your index and middle finger. Turn the plant upside down and allow the medium to rest against your upturned hand.

2 Gently remove the pot.

3 Place the young plant into the larger pot. Add more medium and firm down.

4 Water and feed.

6 CARE AND MAINTENANCE

LIGHTING

You have no doubt gathered by now that lighting is a pretty deep subject. It is a complete science in itself but why is the right kind of light so important for good results?

The best grow light we have is 93 million miles away—sunlight has the perfect spectrum for growing as it is 100 per cent Photosynthetic Active Radiation (P.A.R.). This form of radiation (light) reacts with the surface of the leaf and via the process of photosynthesis creates the energy required for the plant to grow.

High Intensity Discharge

High Intensity Discharge lights are the same type of light that are used in street lighting.

Light is categorized by color or, to be more specific, spectrum. The measure by which color is calculated in horticulture is by way of the "Kelvin" scale, which informs us that the red end of the spectrum is at approximately 2,500 k, with the blue end of the spectrum at 6,100 k.

This effectively means that a light in the red spectrum is good for flowering

Top Tip

Make sure you never use halogen lights to grow weed.

High Intensity Discharge (H.I.D.) lights are available in 250w, 400w, 600w, and 1000w. In the vegging stage lights are on 24/7.

and a blue light is good for vegging.

As described earlier, High Intensity Discharge lighting units consist of a lamp and a reflector connected to a ballast which provides the initial large inductive charge required to power the lamp (bulb).

For vegging purposes the lamp should emit light at the blue end of the spectrum (6,000k+). Metal Halide lamps operate in this range and are ideal for this stage of the plants' growth.

Electricity costs vary; however, power companies generally charge by the kilowatt-hour (kw/h).

A 600w lamp will use 600 watts per hour of operation, this equates to 0.6 kilowatt per hour. Multiply 0.6 by the charge per kw/h (on your bill) and this

will give you an electricity cost per hour. Use this figure to calculate the total weekly running cost of your lights.

I generally find that the 600w H.I.D. light is generally the best all-round choice regarding power and running costs.

The optimum height for the lamps during vegetative growth is to get them as close as possible to the tops of the plants without burning or scorching taking place.

Remember, H.I.D. units will need to have a contactor connected between the ballast and the timer.

Fluorescent Lights

Fluorescent lights are also available in different spectrums. Those operating in the red spectrum are usually referred to as warm and blue fluorescents are called cool.

Blue fluorescents are great for seedlings and cuttings and they can also be used for vegging. Due to the low heat levels produced, the lights can be placed in very close proximity to the plants.

These lights are very cheap to operate.

Top Tip

Using a blue and a red lamp, e.g. combining a High Pressure Sodium and a Metal Halide, together for flowering gives tremendous results.

However, you must ensure that very efficient reflective materials are used in the construction of the grow chamber.

Growers have different motivations and reasons for cultivating cannabis. On the next page are a few examples.

Right: During the vegetative stage, plants should be green and healthy looking. Cannabis plants will vegetate indefinitely unless their exposure to light is changed.

Below: Young cuttings develop well under fluorescent lights.

THE PLANT

Vegetative growth is one of the most important stages in the lifetime of the plant. All growers want big, fat, healthy buds and it is during the vegging stage that the strong, healthy stem and branch structure will form. This will provide a strong chassis on which heavy, fat buds can hang. To supply fuel to support all this rapid growth, a healthy root mass is essential.

There is no set rule as to how long a cannabis plant should vegetate for. Cannabis is a photo-period dependent plant, which means that you can control whether it grows or flowers by adjusting the light and dark period that you expose the plant to. To put it really simply, if you give the plant 18 hours of light and 6 hours of dark, it will grow bigger—if you give it 12 hours of light and 12 hours dark, it will produce buds.

Case Study 1

George

George has converted a small bedroom into a grow room, and harvests 10 plants every two weeks by using the cultivation method Sea of Green, which is often shortened to SOG.

To be in a position to crop 10 plants every two weeks, George needs to plant 10 plants every two weeks as well.

Method used:

George's grow room is, in the main, a flowering room where he operates four High Pressure Sodium lights on a 12 hours on, 12 off cycle.

Within the room George has built a light-proof vegging cabinet where his lights are on 24/7. The cabinet is split into two sections: one contains his Mother plants and cuttings under a blue Envirolite and the other section, where he vegetates the clones for two weeks, uses a 250w Metal Halide.

The flowering area contains 4 trays which in turn contain 10 plants each; over each tray is a 600w High Pressure Sodium lamp. The plants in the trays are at different stages of flowering: two, four, six and eight weeks respectively.

Every two weeks George takes around 20 cuttings from his Mother plants and places them in a propagator under the Envirolite. After two weeks in the propagator they are re-potted and moved to the vegging section of the cabinet under the Metal Halide lamp.

After two weeks of vegetative growth the plants are moved out of the cabinet and into the flowering room.

Summary:

- 10 mature plants are cropped after flowering for 8 weeks.
- They will be replaced by 10 plants that have been vegging for 2 weeks.
- Which in turn will be replaced by 10 rooted clones selected from 20 taken.
- 20 cuttings will be taken from the mothers to continue the cycle.

Top Tip

George takes more cuttings than he needs, which guarantees him at least 10 healthy, strong clones. The excess plants are destroyed.

Lamps hung too close to your plants can cause their tops to burn. Too far away and the plants will stretch.

The plants above have recently been moved from a vegetative state to the flowering room. They will soon show signs of sex.

Case Study 2

Sarah

Sarah grows her own plant and is more concerned with quality than quantity.

Method used:

Sarah has a small Growdrobe set-up containing a couple of plants. She uses a blue 200w Envirolite for vegetative growth and a red one for flowering. Her plants are grown from clones provided by a medical marijuana co-operative and she operates her light for 24/7 during the vegging period.

Being a vegan, she will only use organic nutrients and avoids all chemical fertilizers and pesticides.

She vegetates her plants for four weeks and flowers for eight. This allows her to grow four crops per year and is sufficient for all her needs.

A small closet grow at the end of its vegetative period and about to go into the 12/12 lighting period.

Conclusions

There are many different reasons and motivations for growing cannabis and a multitude of cultivation methods to fulfill your needs and circumstances. Start small, keep it simple, and you will be encouraged by your success. Not only will you have the satisfaction of benefitting from the best quality plants, you will also have discovered an exciting new interest.

NUTRIENTS

Using a food rich in nitrogen as described in Chapter 3 will promote strong, vigorous growth and the leaves should appear a rich, dark green, healthy color.

PHOTO-PERIODS

Especially during your first grow, you will find yourself "checking" on your plants many times during the day. Spending time with your plants is a good thing. However, do it only when the lights are on.

DO NOT BE TEMPTED TO HAVE A LOOK AT THE PLANTS WHEN THE LIGHTS ARE OFF —NEVER INTERRUPT THE DARK PERIOD. WHEN IT IS DARK, LET IT STAY DARK.

It has long been thought that night-time and darkness were important to plants, which is why the majority of cannabis cultivators choose a daily lighting period of 18 hours on and 6 off.

However, some growers prefer to operate their lights 24 hours a day during the vegging period as they believe nothing is gained by having a lights off period in the vegging stage.

Personally, I believe the plants benefit from having a daily rest.

When the lights are operating the plants absorb CO_2 from the air. During the dark period, the process is reversed and the plant takes in oxygen from the atmosphere and gives off CO_2 in return. As a grower you should take advantage of this by allowing a 20-minute extractor fan delay when the lights are switched on—this allows the plants to re-absorb the CO_2 from the now CO2-rich environment.

> ### Top Tip
>
> If the humidity level drops below 50 per cent you can raise the level by hanging wet towels in the vegging area when the lights are operating.

TIME

The length of the vegging period will vary depending on the cultivation method being used—the longer the time the larger the plant will grow.

Indoor grow rooms usually have height restrictions, so as a rough guide veg your plants until they reach a third of the height of your lights, then change to the flowering stage. Obviously the final height of the mature plant is also dependent on the genetics of the variety being cultivated.

PRUNING

One of the most commonly used pruning methods is known as "topping." This is the process of "pinching out" the main growing tip at the top of the central stem.

This process will temporarily slow the upward growth and will encourage side growth by taking advantage of the fact that the stem immediately below the pinched part will produce two new shoots. These two new stems in turn can have their growing tips removed, and so on. However, some strains such as Ice do not respond well to this process and topping is best left until you have a crop or two completed.

Also, do not be tempted to remove any of the large fan leaves from the plant in the belief that the removal of these leaves will enable more light to reach the lower branches of the plant and increase the yield. The fan leaves are the "lungs" of the plant and their presence is essential to its wellbeing. They should only ever be removed if they are discolored or sickly looking.

The plants in this grow chamber are flourishing under the 18/6 light cycle. Never be tempted to interrupt the plants' dark period during this stage.

7

FLOWERING

LIGHTING

High Intensity Discharge

In order to provide the correct spectrum for flowering, a H.I.D. lighting unit will need to be fitted with a High Pressure Sodium lamp. The red light emitted by the HPS lamp promotes a greater flower-to-leaf ratio than Metal Halide or Fluorescent lights.

Fluorescent Lights and Envirolites

The addition of a blue Envirolite or "cool" type fluorescent as supplementary lighting when using a HPS for flowering, will result in more vigorous growth and the formation of tight, compact, hard buds.

Red Envirolites can be used for flowering on their own or to supplement HPS lighting.

THE FLOWERING PLANT

The cannabis cultivator triggers the flowering process by controlling and manipulating the photoperiod. In nature, longer nights signal to the cannabis plant that winter is approaching and it is time to flower and commence seed production to ensure that the species survives.

Outdoors the photoperiod changes with the passing of the seasons. In the

Flowering cannabis plants in a Sea of Green set-up.

During the flowering period the plant will divert her energies to bud production. This plant is showing the early signs of flowering.

branch, and stem production to flower production.

At the end of the first week of flowering, check the plants to confirm that they are all females, and remove and destroy any males.

During weeks four to five, remove the lower, poorly formed, wispy looking flowers known as "air buds." This will enable the plant to put all of its energy and efforts into developing the buds of the upper canopy.

Northern Hemisphere the longest day occurs around June 21. From then onward the length of the day gradually decreases until it reaches its shortest duration on or around December 22. The day length then starts to gradually increase until the cycle is completed around June 21.

Due to the tilt of the Earth on its axis, the length of the day is also affected by where on the Earth you happen to be. As you move toward the equator, changes in the photoperiod are less drastic over the course of the year. For example, on the Equator the day length is around 12 hours on June 21 and 11 hours on December 22. Maine is 45 degrees north of the Equator and here the day length varies between 16 hours in June and falls to less than 9 hours in December.

In the northerly latitudes cannabis is prevented from flowering until late in the year, which can be a problem if the crop cannot be harvested before the onset of winter.

Wherever you happen to be on the planet, cannabis grown outside will commence flowering when the daylight has shortened to 12 hours. The photoperiod required for flowering will vary slightly depending on the variety, the age of the plant, and the environment.

When you decide that the time is right to commence flowering in your grow room, program the timer to switch the lights on for a 12-hour period per day. This is commonly known as 12/12.

When the plant commences flowering, she transfers the emphasis from leaf,

During the later stages of flowering buds, and trim leaves will become covered in resin. This plant will soon be ready for harvest.

Top Tip

During the lights off (or dark period), do not enter the grow room.

SUPPORT

Supporting the branches and the main stem helps the plant resist buckling and bending under the weight of the mature buds.

If you use a trellis for support it should be put in place during the vegetative stage. Attempting to add it during the later stages of flower can cause damage. Allowing the plant and the buds to grow through the trellis is the recommended course of action.

A simple trellis arrangement provides good support and protection to the flowering plants, especially prior to harvest when the buds are full and heavy.

FEEDING

During the flowering stage the plant will require lower levels of nitrogen and higher levels of phosphorous.

The extra phosphorous will encourage and promote flower production which means big, fat, heavy buds!

Use a fertilizer with an NPK of 15-30-30.

Right: Plants will generally benefit from support, especially when buds are nearing maturity. Simple supports like this trellis work very well.

Opposite: Tall plants can be gently bent away from the light and held down with twine.

HARVESTING

HARVESTING

When to harvest is a matter of personal choice and experience. A common indicator of maturity is the color of the pistils. As a general rule, when approximately 70 per cent of the pistils have turned from white to red in color the plant is ready for harvesting.

It is generally agreed amongst growers that the ideal and more precise indicator of the optimum time to harvest is the color of the glandular trichomes. Simply, this means that the clearer the trichome color the more cerebral the high; the cloudier (milkier) the trichome the more of a body effect or body stone.

A microscope or a jeweler's loupe (ideal magnification around x30) is an essential piece of equipment; this will enable you to choose the optimum time for harvesting.

On your first grow it would be worth cropping individual sample buds (or individual plants) when their pistils are 50 per cent, 70 per cent, and 100 per cent turned. Closely examine the three samples with your microscope (or jeweler's loupe) and note the differences in the color and translucency of the trichomes. Clearly label the three bud samples and dry them using the methods described later in this chapter.

Having decided that the time is right to harvest the fruits of your labor, you can harvest complete plants or individual buds. The upper canopy of the plants

Above: This plant will soon be ready for harvesting. Using a loupe to assess the trichomes will help you determine the optimum time.

Right: You can also check buds with your fingers for signs of maturity. The stickier the bud, the better.

receive more light and they will generally mature earlier than the lower canopy where the buds receive less light. Some growers prefer to harvest individual buds rather than the whole plant and they will remove the upper mature buds and allow the lower buds to continue flowering until they have matured.

If you decide to harvest the whole plant, cut the main stem close to the medium. Cannabis stems are very tough and you must take care if using scissors; a knife with a serrated edge (e.g. steak knife) is a far safer option.

Top Tip

For your first harvest, cut down one plant (or bud) when 50 per cent of the pistils have turned from white to red and allow the remaining plants to continue flowering. When 70 per cent of the pistils have turned red, crop all but one plant (or bud). Allow the remaining plant (or bud) to develop until 90 to 100 per cent of the pistils have turned red, then crop. Once they are dry, smoking these samples in a pipe (without tobacco) will give an indication of how cropping at different stages of maturity can affect the high.

Whole plants can be harvested by cutting the main stem approximately 1 inch (2.5cm) above the medium.

DRYING

The slower and the longer the drying process the better the quality of the end product. Slow drying allows chlorophyll to be dispersed and this will greatly improve the taste and flavor of the end product. To have reached the drying stage is a great achievement and you will soon be rewarded for all your time and effort. Do not be tempted to speed up the drying process with dehumidifiers or excess heat.

It is understandable that you will be in a hurry to sample your harvest. In an emergency, fresh buds can be quickly dried by placing them on a radiator or by spreading them out on a baking tray and putting them in a warm oven. However, these methods are not recommended, as quick drying tends to results in a "harsh" smoke. It is better to have patience and allow nature to take its course.

If you have the luxury of spare space in your grow room you can construct a drying chamber. The advantage of having your drying chamber within your grow room is that you do not need an additional carbon filter. If you construct a drying chamber outside of your grow room, a carbon filter attached to an extraction fan is essential to eliminate any odor.

Whether your drying area is a purpose-built cupboard or even just a large cardboard box, the addition of an

Suspending harvested buds from twine allows the air to circulate freely during the drying process and helps to prevent bud rot.

extraction fan will enable the removal of stale humid air. Inlet holes should be bored near the base of the drying cupboard to allow fresh air to enter.

The air should be changed approximately every two hours and a conventional shower or kitchen-type fan operated via a timer will normally suffice. However, if

Top Tips

• A small desk fan can assist the drying process by circulating the air within the drying chamber.

• Instead of using tobacco in joints, fan leaves can be dried and used as a substitute.

your drying chamber is outside of your grow room then an inline fan attached to a carbon filter should be used.

Strong twine or wire coat hangers can be used to support the drying buds. Some growers prefer to use screen racks or shelves for the drying process, but this can lead to "flat spots" on the bud.

The ideal environment for drying is cool and dark with humidity levels below 50 per cent and temperature ranging between 60–75°F (15–24°C).

A combined thermometer and hygrometer with a maximum and minimum memory is essential to ensure optimum drying conditions.

Remove all the large fan leaves and hang the plants or buds upside down. I prefer to hang individual branches rather than the complete plant as this allows air to circulate more freely.

Large fan leaves can be removed either before or after cropping.

Plants should be allowed to hang freely. Do not allow buds or plants to touch each other (or the sides of the chamber) as this will impair the drying process and could allow bud rot to gain a foothold.

Check your drying plants every day. Gently squeezing a bud will allow you to assess the drying process. You should feel a difference in the texture and the feel of the bud as the drying process continues.

Examine sample buds from different areas of your drying chamber and look for signs of bud rot. If there are any signs of rot then remove the damaged bud immediately and reduce the humidity within the chamber by increasing the exchange of air within the chamber.

After seven days the buds should have lost a fair amount of moisture and they should feel lighter and drier. The buds should now be given a very close manicure. The small leaves removed from the drying buds in the manicuring process are called "trim." The trim leaves can be stored in the freezer for later use in tinctures, cooking, or hash making; small buds from the lower canopy can also be removed in the manicuring process.

A purpose-built drying chamber offers control over the drying process. Ensure your buds are well spaced out within the chamber.

Left: After seven days of drying the buds should feel a lot lighter. At this point the buds can be removed from their branches and manicured: that is, all excess trim leaves removed.

Below: Air buds and trim leaves—the waste product from the trimming process—are nevertheless still high in THC content. This "waste" can be dried completely and used for hash making.

When you are manicuring, you may find yourself with an unbelievably sticky coating on your fingers and scissors. This is almost pure resin, otherwise known as finger hash and is the ultimate hash!

Drying times will obviously vary from environment to environment and will even vary at different times of the year, so it is impossible to give a total drying time. If the buds have been allowed to dry too quickly they will feel dry on the outside and damp inside where the stem is, and this can lead to bud rot. Correctly dried cannabis bud will contain approximately 15 per cent moisture.

Take a bud, hold it with both hands at eye level and bend both ends of the stem downward. If the stem creases without splitting, then it will require additional drying. If the stem snaps cleanly in two then it has been over-dried. The optimum moisture content of 15 per cent has been achieved when the central stem half breaks, i.e. the outside of the stem will split but the central core of the stem will hold it all together.

If you inadvertently over-dry your bud, seal it in an airtight container with a fresh fan leaf and leave overnight—this will re-hydrate your weed.

Right: Hold a stem and bend slowly.

Below: If the stem "half breaks" the bud has a moisture content of about 15 per cent and is ready for curing.

CURING

Why cure? Very few growers of cannabis will bother to cure their produce. However, if you wish to produce cannabis of the highest quality, then curing is absolutely essential.

After investing time and money in setting yourself up with the knowledge and equipment to produce your own bananas, would you consume them before they were ripe? If a freshly harvested banana is stored under the correct conditions it will with time ripen to perfection, as will cannabis.

During the curing process terpenes in the bud will isomerize into polyterpenes which will produce the mellow taste and flavor associated with the highest quality cannabis favored by the true connoisseur.

Re-hydrate over-dried bud by adding a freshly picked fan leaf to the curing jar and leave overnight.

Top Tip

Heat, light, and exposure to air will degrade THC. Store your cannabis in airtight containers somewhere dark and cool.

How to cure

Loosely place the buds in a Kilner jar or plastic airtight container until it is approximately 80 per cent full. This loose packing of the buds allows air to circulate within the jar.

For the first few weeks, open the tops of the jar for five to ten minutes per day to allow the stale air in the jar to be replaced by fresh air. This action, known as burping, will avoid a build-up of moisture, which could result in the development of molds or fungus.

Left: Bud can be stored in this way for many months and even years! Fine wines and whiskeys benefit from ageing and so does cannabis.

Right: Cured weed has a mellow taste and flavor, with none of the back of the throat "nitrate" burn associated with fast-dried and uncured dealer weed.

REGENERATION

If you have no access to clones or seeds to replace your mature crop, then the regeneration of your cannabis plant could be a good option.

To regenerate a cannabis plant, remove the upper buds from a mature plant but allow the stems, fan leaves, and the lower buds to remain.

Place the plant under 24 hours of (blue) light and feed with a food with a high nitrogen content. If you are growing hydroponically, drain the bloom solution in the reservoir and refill with a grow nutrient solution.

In ten days or so you should notice some new growth; allow the plant to vegetate and then flower as normal. This process can be repeated many times.

Regeneration is ideal for those growers without access to clones or seeds. This plant is pictured after a month of regenerating.

TROUBLESHOOTING

9

PESTS

There is nothing more frustrating for the cannabis grower than to successfully cultivate plants, only to have the crop killed by a pest infestation. This section outlines some of the more common bugs and pests that are to be avoided.

Aphids, commonly known as greenfly and blackfly, feed on plant sap; they also transmit many plant viruses.

These tiny black flies are about 2mm in length and are often seen running over the plants. Pale-colored larvae with shiny black heads emerge from eggs planted in the rooting medium. These larvae then feed on the roots and tunnel into the stems of new cuttings, often killing the plants.

Whitefly resemble small, moth-like pests. Check the underside of leaves for signs of eggs. As the plants grow, the eggs hatch into scale-like larvae that are unable to move. Both adult and juvenile whiteflies feed on plant sap and produce copious amounts of honeydew, which promotes the growth of sooty molds.

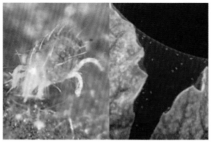

Spidermites are a serious problem for the indoor and outdoor cannabis cultivator. White spots on the tops of leaves and a fine webbing usually indicate the presence of this pest. Careful examination of the affected area will reveal the mites as small, yellowy-brown dots crawling over the leaf surface. These tiny, sap-sucking pests thrive in hot, dry weather.

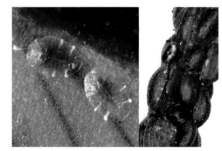

Scale insects suck sap from plants; some excrete honeydew, which makes sticky, sooty molds. They are hidden under waxy shells or scales.

Mealybugs produce groups of 100–400 eggs protected under a layer of waxy threads. They reduce plant growth and cause leaves to distort.

Thrips are just over 1mm in length and are sometimes referred to as "Thunder flies." They feed on pollen and sap. Adult females lay eggs in a slit cut into a leaf.

COMMON ENVIRONMENTAL DEFICIENCIES

- **Stretchy plants**—Tall, elongated, stretched plants are usually caused by having the cultivation light too far above the plant.
- **Clones**—Yellowing leaves on un-rooted clones can be caused by too much light intensity. Use fluorescent lights.
- **Mold and Fungus**—Usually caused by high humidity levels. Increase the amount of ventilation by increasing the speed of the fan or have it on for longer periods. Check all the plants for signs of mold or fungus and remove any dead or damaged leaves.
- **Heat**—If your lights are too close to the plants, the uppermost leaves will be prone to curling and they will look burnt. Raise the lights and direct a circulation fan toward the lamp. Avoid exposing your plants to temperatures above 86°F (30°C) for long periods.

- **Cold**—Cold temperatures (below 50°F/ 10°C) slow the growth rate. If you are using a hydroponic system, the use of a fish tank heater in the reservoir tank will keep the roots of the plant warm.

Above and below: Powdery mildew causes a white growth across the surface of the leaves.

Above: Botrytis (Budrot) is the scourge of the grower.

CANNABIS NUTRIENT DISORDERS

Nutrient disorders are caused by too much or too little of one or several nutrients being available. These nutrients are made available between a pH range of 5 and 7 and a total dissolved solids (TDS) range of 800 to 3000 PPM. Maintaining these conditions is the key to proper nutrient uptake.

Over twenty elements are needed for a plant to grow. Carbon, hydrogen, and oxygen are absorbed from the air and water. The rest of the elements, called mineral nutrients, are dissolved in the nutrient solution. The primary or macro-nutrients (nitrogen (N), phosphorus (P) and potassium (K) are the elements plants use the most. Calcium (Ca) and magnesium (Mg) are secondary nutrients and used in smaller amounts. Iron (Fe), sulfur (S), manganese (Mn), boron (B), molybdenum (Mo), zinc (Zn) and copper (Cu) are micro-nutrients or trace elements. Trace elements are found in most soils. Rockwool (hydroponic) fertilizers must contain these trace elements, as they do not normally exist in sufficient quantities in Rockwool or water. **NOTE:** The nutrients must be soluble and go into the solution.

Macro-nutrients
Nitrogen (N) is primary to plant growth. Plants convert nitrogen to make the proteins essential to new cell growth.

Nitrogen is mainly responsible for leaf and stem growth as well as overall size and vigor. Nitrogen moves easily to active young buds, shoots, and leaves and slower to older leaves. Deficiency signs show first in older leaves. They turn a pale yellow and may die. New growth becomes weak and spindly. An abundance of nitrogen will cause soft, weak growth and even delay flower and fruit production if it is allowed to accumulate.

Phosphorus (P) is necessary for photosynthesis and works as a catalyst for energy transfer within the plant. Phosphorus helps build strong roots and is vital for flower and seed production.

Highest levels of phosphorus are used during germination, seedling growth, and flowering. Deficiencies will show in older leaves first. Leaves turn deep green on a uniformly smaller, stunted plant. Leaves show brown or purple spots.
NOTE: Phosphorus flocculates when concentrated and combined with calcium.

Potassium (K) activates the manufacture and movement of sugars and starches, as well as growth by cell division. Potassium increases chlorophyll in foliage and helps regulate stomata openings so plants make better use of light and air. Potassium encourages strong root growth and water uptake and triggers enzymes that fight disease. Potassium is necessary during all stages of growth. Deficiency

The major discoloring of this leaf indicates an advanced stage of nitrogen deficiency.

signs of potassium are: Older leaves mottle and yellow between veins, followed by whole leaves that turn dark yellow and die. Flower drop is a common problem associated with potassium deficiency. Potassium is usually locked out by high salinity.

Magnesium (Mg) is found as a central atom in the chlorophyll molecule and is essential to the absorption of light energy. Magnesium aids in the utilization of nutrients, and neutralizes acids and toxic compounds produced by the plant. Deficiency signs of magnesium are: Older leaves yellow from the center outward, while veins remain green on deficient plants. Leaf tips and edges may discolor and curl upward. Growing tips turn lime green if the deficiency progresses to the top of the plant.

Calcium (Ca) is fundamental to cell manufacture and growth. Soil gardeners use dolomite lime, which contains calcium and magnesium, to keep the soil sweet or buffered. Rockwool gardeners use calcium to buffer excess nutrients. Calcium moves slowly within the plant and tends to concentrate in roots and older growth. Consequently, young growth shows deficiency signs first. Deficient leaf tips, edges and new growth will turn brown and die back. If too much calcium is applied early in life, it will stunt growth as well. It will also flocculate when a concentrated form is combined with potassium.

Trace Elements

Sulfur (S) is a component of plant proteins and plays a role in root growth and chlorophyll supply. Sulfur, like calcium, moves little within plant tissue and the first signs of a deficiency are pale young leaves. Growth is slow but leaves tend to be brittle and stay narrower than normal.

Iron (Fe) is a key catalyst in chlorophyll production and is used in photosynthesis. A lack of iron turns leaves pale yellow or white while the veins remain green. Iron is difficult for plants to absorb and moves slowly within the plant. Always use iron in nutrient mixes.

Manganese (Mn) works with plant enzymes to reduce nitrates before producing proteins. A lack of manganese turns young leaves a mottled yellow/brown.

Zinc (Z) is a catalyst and must be present in minute amounts for plant growth. A lack of zinc results in stunting, yellowing, and curling of small leaves.

Copper (Cu) is a catalyst for several enzymes. A shortage of copper makes new growth wilt and causes irregular growth. Excess copper causes sudden death. Copper is also used as a fungicide and wards off insects and diseases.

Boron (B) is necessary for cells to divide, and protein formation. It also

Top Tip

Magnesium deficiency is pretty common as cannabis uses a lot of it and many fertilizers do not contain enough of it.
Mg deficiency is easily fixed with a tablespoon per gallon solution of stomach-settling salts (first powdered and dissolved in some hot water).

plays an active role in pollination and seed production.

Molybdenum (Mo) helps form proteins and aids the plant's ability to fix nitrogen from the air. A deficiency causes leaves to turn pale, and fringes to appear scorched. Irregular leaf growth may also result.

These nutrients are mixed together to form a complete plant fertilizer to give plants all they need for lush, rapid growth.

Water transports these soluble nutrients into contact with the plant roots. In the presence of oxygen and water, the nutrients are absorbed through the root hairs.

10

UTILIZE

WHAT IS HASH AND HOW DO I MAKE IT?

Hashish, more commonly shortened to "hash", is the generic name for the solid concentrated form of cannabis which is produced by processing the glandular trichomes extracted from the cannabis plant. There are many forms of hash, with a huge variance in colour, taste, and aroma, from the high-quality, heavy, sedative Nepalese Temple Balls to the poor-quality Moroccan "Soapbar."

The differences between the various forms of hashish are determined by the methods used in its preparation. The production process can be divided into two main parts—resin collection and resin preparation.

Sieving

Plants are first dried and then agitated or rubbed lightly against mesh or cloth screens of varying sizes. This process allows trichomes and other plant debris to fall off the plant and pass through the screens onto a collection surface.

The finer the mesh and the less force used in the process then the higher the quality; more force and a larger mesh size allows more plant matter to be collected and therefore the quality is reduced.

The raw resin powder can be compressed into a solid form by applying pressure, either by hand or by mechanical means. The application of pressure will generate heat, which aids the bonding process.

Water and ice collection

This works on the basis that cannabis trichomes are insoluble in water and at 2°C they are very brittle. The agitation of bud and trim leaves in freezing water will allow the trichomes to break off from the plant material. If this mixture of freezing water and cannabis material is passed through a series of mesh bags (graded by screen size) differing grades can be collected. The finer the mesh, the finer the quality. A 25 micron screen will produce a very fine-quality hash.

There are various ice extraction systems available; bag systems contain two to seven bags and can be purchased from good-quality cultivation stores.

A basic bag set will consist of a catching bag containing a screen size in the region of 190 micron. This bag is designed to "catch" the plant material and the finer filtration bags will filter the trichomes from the water; the smaller the mesh the less plant material will pass through and therefore the higher the quality of the hash.

The bags need to be placed in the mixing bucket in the correct order. The smallest sized screen (the finest) is placed in the bucket first, the remaining bags are placed inside each other in order of size. The final bag is the one with the largest size mesh (the coarsest) and this will hold the plant material and is where the mixing will take place.

1 Place the bags into your mixing bucket—the bag with the finest screen goes in first. The catching bag will contain the coarsest screen and is the final bag.

2 Having first put your trim in a freezer for a couple of hours, transfer it to the container. Half fill the bucket with water.

3 Top up the bucket with cold water until the bucket is two-thirds full and add lots of ice. The temperature of the water has to be below 39°F (4°C). Keep adding ice and check the temperature at regular intervals throughout the process.

4 Use an electric whisk to agitate the cold water for 15 minutes. The mixing process will cause the cold, brittle trichomes to break off the plant material.

5 After mixing, place the bucket in a fridge or even outside if it is cold, and allow to settle for 30 minutes. Remove the catching bag from the bucket. Allow the bag to drain and place on one side, then do the same with the remaining bags.

6 After the water has drained from the bag, you are left with lovely trichomes.

7 An example of the type of hash you are left with (above).

The pressing process

Once you have your hash in semi-solidified form it needs to be pressed. The hand-pressing process is best carried out over a large plate or clean, hard surface.

Ensure your hands are clean. Wash thoroughly, scrubbing if necessary, and use an unscented soap.

1 Work your thumb into your other two fingers and you will feel the powder begin to "lump" together. The resin will warm and start to stick to your fingers.

2 Continue to work the piece between your fingers, the lumps will begin to increase in size as they bond together. As the pressure and heat generated by the hand-pressing process increases, the delicate trichomes burst, resulting in a darkening of the color.

3 After 10 minutes or so the lumps will bond into a single mass.

4 By now the mixture should be easily manipulated into a sausage shape and be dark brown in color.

5 Continue to roll and work the hash between your fingers into a ball.

THE MUNCHIES

Smoking pot is renowned for stimulating the appetite and bringing on attacks of the munchies. By happy coincidence, these cravings offer dedicated potheads a further opportunity for consuming cannabis— by cooking it up in various tasty recipes.

However, when cooking with cannabis, certain provisos should be borne in mind. Firstly, the effects of eating it are not as instantaneous or as quantifiable as when smoking it. It takes longer to come on than smoking—sometimes up to a couple of hours. And when it does finally arrive, the effect is going to be a good deal stronger and longer. Often the effects of eating can last for up to 12 hours and will keep coming back in waves. Some find this experience scary and overwhelming. They say they feel more comfortable and in control of the situation when they smoke it.

And, of course, it goes without saying that it is totally out of order to ever spike anyone's food with dope without first obtaining their express consent. If, however, in spite of all this, you do decide to go ahead and give cooking with cannabis a go, at least be sure to err on the side of caution and keep individual intakes down to no more than a few joints-worth per sitting.

Majoon

Pot is particularly suitable for use in sweet recipes and those involving lashings of chocolate.

This has long been recognized. The ancient Arabs and Persians were particularly fond of using it to make majoon—an Arab word meaning sweetmeats laced with cannabis. A typical majoon might take the form of Turkish delight. Common ingredients used in making majoon confections included sugar, milk, cocoa butter, honey, crushed nuts, and dried fruits.

The 19th-century potheads of Europe and America also chose to eat, rather than smoke, cannabis and would frequently employ sweetened preparations to mask its flavor. Cannabis featured in various medical tinctures of the time too—its psychoactive THC content being extracted by soaking it in alcohol.

One of the many common misconceptions about cannabis is that its psychoactive THC component can be extracted by boiling it in water. This is not the case. In fact, its THC content can only be extracted by using fats, oils, or alcohol.

Each of the following recipes uses cannabis in its raw and natural state, prepared in conjunction with various fats and oils. However, for those intending to cook with cannabis on a regular basis it will probably make more sense to make up a batch of cannabis-laced "space butter" to dip into whenever the occasion arises.

Top Tip

Ingesting cannabis is totally different to smoking it, the effects take more time to be felt and last longer.

Canna butter

This is the main ingredient in almost all cannabis cooking. Its earthy, slightly bitter taste is best masked by using it in recipes requiring lots of chocolate, cinnamon, or ginger.

8 OZ/2 STICKS (250G) UNSALTED BUTTER

4 PINTS (2.5 LITRES) WATER

1 OZ (25G) WET OR DRY TRIM LEAF

1 Take a large pan and add the water. Add the trim leaf and stir. Bring to the boil. Reduce the heat and allow to gently simmer.

2 Add the butter and stir until completely dissolved. Allow to simmer for 3 hours, stirring every 30 minutes.

3 Stretch 3 or 4 layers of cheesecloth (or muslin) over a large pan. Scoop out the trim and place it on the cloth. Pour the contents of the pan over the shake (gloves should be worn as the mixture is quite hot).

4 Pour boiling water from a kettle over the trim to wash off any remaining butter residue. Carefully squeeze the cloth to remove all the butter and throw away the shake (caution, it is still quite hot).

5 Pour the butter and water mixture into a plastic container. Place in the refrigerator overnight.

6 As the butter and water separate, the butter will rise to the surface and solidify.

7 Skim off the butter and store in the refrigerator.

Cannabis Chocolate

This is a recipe for home-made cannabis chocolate. For best results, make sure the cannabis is as finely ground as possible.

5 OZ (150G) BAR OF CHOCOLATE, BROKEN INTO PIECES

$^1/_8$ OZ (3.5G) GOOD-QUALITY BUD

1 Place a glass bowl in a pan of water on a hot plate. Place the chocolate into the bowl. Using the bowl inside the pan of water creates a double boiler. This ensures the chocolate is not heated excessively. Do not use a microwave to melt the chocolate, this will cause burning.

2 Finely chop the bud in a coffee grinder—the finer ground the better. Ideally, the ground cannabis should resemble a very fine dust.

3 When the heated chocolate resembles a thick liquid with no lumps, slowly add the ground bud. Stir well to ensure equal distribution throughout the chocolate.

4 Carefully remove the bowl from the pan (take care, it will be hot) and pour into an ice cube tray. When the chocolate is set, push out the cubes and keep in tin foil or a plastic container in the refrigerator.

Potty pizza

Although traditionally consumed in sweet dishes, cannabis is perfect for spicing up pizza, the hash or grass blending in well with the other earthy flavors.

FOR THE DOUGH:

13 OZ/3 1/2 CUPS (400G) PLAIN FLOUR, PLUS EXTRA FOR COATING

1 OZ (25G) YEAST

1 TSP SUGAR

8 FL OZ (250ML) WARM WATER

1 TSP SALT

2 TBSPS OLIVE OIL

FOR THE TOPPING:

OLIVE OIL FOR FRYING

1 LARGE ONION, FINELY SLICED

1 LARGE RED PEPPER

1/4 OZ (8G) FINELY CRUMBLED HASH, OR 1/2 OZ (16G) GROUND BUD

6 OZ (175G) FINELY SLICED MUSHROOMS

1 CAN OF PLUM TOMATOES, DRAINED AND FINELY CHOPPED

8 OZ/2 CUPS (250G) GRATED SWISS OR ITALIAN CHEESE

12 STONED OLIVES

MAKES 2 LARGE PIZZAS

1 To make the dough, sift the flour into a bowl. Scoop out a well in the center and crumble in the yeast and sugar. Then add the water, knead into a heavy dough, cover with a cloth and leave in a warm place to rise for 30 minutes. Then add the salt and oil. Beat into a smooth paste with a wooden spoon. Knead into a ball, coat with flour, and set to one side.

2 For the topping, gently fry the red pepper and onion in oil. Gradually add in the sliced mushrooms and the hash or grass. Gently cook for 5 to 10 minutes.

3 Roll out the pizza dough into two circular bases. Spread the tomatoes over the dough and then add the onion and mushroom topping. Sprinkle with olives and grated cheese. Grill or bake in a hot oven (425°F/220°C/Gas 7) for around 10 minutes.

Chocolate nut space fudge

The *Alice B Toklas Cook Book* of 1954 scandalized readers by including a recipe for hashish fudge, which she dubbed the "food of paradise." This is a variation on the original recipe.

4 OZ/1 STICK (125G) UNSALTED BUTTER

4 TBSPS BLACK COFFEE

2 TBSPS COCOA POWDER

2 TBSPS GOLDEN SYRUP

1 1/4 LB/5 CUPS (625G) CASTER SUGAR

3/4 OZ (20G) CRUMBLED HASH, OR 1 1/2 OZ (40G) GROUND BUDS

7 FL OZ (200ML) CONDENSED MILK

4 OZ/1 CUP (125G) CHOPPED PECAN NUTS

1 Grease an 11 x 7 inch (28 x 18cm) baking tin.

2 Melt the butter in a large pan and gradually stir in the hash or grass. Then add the coffee, cocoa, syrup, and sugar. Heat gently, stirring occasionally until the sugar has dissolved. Do not allow to boil at this stage or the finished fudge will crystalize and lack the desired smooth texture.

3 Add the condensed milk and bring to the boil, stirring. Boil steadily for 5 to 10 minutes, until the bubbles become more volcanic.

4 Turn off the heat and wait until the bubbling subsides. Then whisk briskly for about 5 minutes, until the mixture becomes smoother and more glutinous.

5 Add the chopped nuts and mix them in well. Pour the mix onto the prepared baking tin and leave for 30 minutes until semi-set. Mark into 1 inch (2.5cm) squares with a sharp knife and then leave to fully chill and set.

6 Finally, cut into squares and store in a cool place in biscuit tins.

Magic mocha brownies

This classic cannabis recipe is great as a comfort food in winter and as an energy booster on activity holidays. You'll feel capable of taking (or toking) on Everest.

4 OZ (125G) DARK CHOCOLATE

2 OZ/$\frac{1}{2}$ STICK (50G) UNSALTED BUTTER

$\frac{1}{2}$ OZ (15G) CRUMBLED HASH OR 1 OZ (25G) FINELY GROUND BUD

6 OZ/1 CUP (175G) DARK, SOFT, BROWN SUGAR

2 EGGS

1 TBSPN STRONG BLACK COFFEE (COLD)

6 OZ/1 CUP (175G) PLAIN FLOUR

$\frac{1}{2}$ TSP BAKING POWDER

PINCH OF SALT

2 OZ/$\frac{1}{2}$ CUP (50G) CHOPPED WALNUTS, PECANS, OR BRAZIL NUTS

MAKES 16 BROWNIES

1 Preheat oven to 350°F/180°C/Gas 4.
Grease and line an 8 inch (20cm) square cake tin.

2 Melt the chocolate, butter, and hash or grass in a large pan over low heat, then set aside to cool down.

3 Beat the sugar and eggs together in a deep bowl until thick and pale. Fold in the melted chocolate mix and the cold coffee. Mix thoroughly. Sift in the flour, baking powder, and salt. Lightly fold into mixture. Then add the chopped nuts.

4 Pour the mixture into your prepared tin and bake in the oven for 25 to 30 minutes. Your brownies are done when firm and when an inserted fork comes out clean. Leave them to semi-cool for 30 minutes before cutting into squares. Store the brownies in a cool, dry place.

Scooby snacks

Named after cartoon canine hero Scooby Doo. Why? Because scooby rhymes with doobie. With snacks like these around, it's really no wonder he always had the munchies.

4 OZ/1 STICK (125G) UNSALTED BUTTER

2 OZ/5 TBSP (50G) GRANULATED SUGAR

2 OZ (50G) LIGHT SOFT BROWN SUGAR

$\frac{1}{2}$ OZ (15G) CRUMBLED HASH, OR 1 OZ (25G) GROUND GANJA

1 EGG

FEW DROPS VANILLA ESSENCE

4 OZ/1 CUP (125G) PLAIN FLOUR

$\frac{1}{2}$ OZ (15G) COCOA POWDER

$\frac{1}{2}$ TSP BICARBONATE OF SODA

4OZ/$\frac{2}{3}$ CUP (125G) PLAIN DARK CHOCOLATE CHIPS

2OZ/$\frac{1}{2}$ CUP (50G) ROUGHLY CHOPPED PECAN NUTS

MAKES ABOUT 30

1 Preheat oven to 350°F/180°C/Gas 4.
Grease 3 baking sheets.

2 Cream the butter, sugars, and cannabis in a bowl until light and fluffy. In another bowl, beat the egg and vanilla essence together. Gradually beat the egg mix into the butter mix.

3 Next, sift the flour, cocoa, and bicarbonate of soda over the creamed mixture, stirring it in carefully. Finally, add the choc chips and nuts.

4 Transfer teaspoon-sized dollops of the mixture onto the pre-prepared baking sheets, spacing the dollops well apart. Then bake in the oven for about 15 minutes until the mixture has spread out and the cookies are beginning to feel firm.

5 Remove from the oven and place on wire racks to cool and crisp. Store the Scooby snacks in an airtight container somewhere dark and cool.

Sleepy-head hot chocolate

A steaming cup of this at bedtime is guaranteed to spread a delightful langor through tired limbs and infuse your inner self with a sense of well-being. Sweet dreams.

2 OZ (50G) GOOD-QUALITY DARK CHOCOLATE SUCH AS VALRHONA

    MANJARI

$\frac{1}{16}$ OZ (2G) GOOD-QUALITY HASH, PREFERABLY BLACK

2 FL OZ (50ML) SINGLE CREAM

10 FL OZ (300ML) FULL-FAT MILK

TO SERVE:

WHIPPED CREAM

GRATED CHOCOLATE

ENOUGH FOR 2 CUPS

1 Break up the chocolate into small pieces. Heat the hash with a flame and crumble into the smallest pieces possible, as if making a joint. Put the chocolate, hash, and cream into a pan and stir over a medium heat until it melts.

2 Meanwhile, bring the milk to the boil in another saucepan and then pour over the melted chocolate. Briskly whisk for a while to stop a skin forming. Serve with whipped cream and grated chocolate.

Mellow yellow ice cream

Gently heating cannabis with cream is an extremely efficient way of maximizing the extraction of its psychoactive THC component. To get the best results, you should really use hash rather than grass.

1OZ/ $\frac{1}{4}$ STICK (25G) BUTTER

18 FL OZ (575ML) SINGLE CREAM

3 OZ/3 TBSPNS (75G) SUGAR

PINCH SALT

$\frac{1}{4}$ OZ (8G) CRUMBLED HASH

15 OZ (450G) BANANAS

3 TBSPNS RUM

5 TBSPNS HONEY

1OZ/ $\frac{1}{4}$ CUP (25G) CHOPPED WALNUTS

SERVES 6

1 Heat the cream in a saucepan until nearly boiling. In a second saucepan melt the butter with the sugar and salt. Heat the hash with a flame and crumble it into the melted butter, stirring all the while. Then whisk in the cream with the butter.

2 Peel the bananas. Put them into a large bowl and mash with a fork. Add the cream, rum, honey, and walnuts. Beat well to mix. Pour the mixture into a chilled, shallow, plastic container. Cover and freeze for a couple of hours until the mixture is mushy in consistency. Turn out the mixture into a chilled bowl. Beat with a metal fork or whisk until smooth.

3 Return the mixture to container, cover and freeze until firm. Transfer to the refrigerator 30 minutes before serving to soften. Serve in scoops in individual glasses with cookies.

MEDICINAL USE

Up until 1940 the United States Pharmacopoeia listed cannabis as a recommended treatment for over one hundred illnesses and diseases, including: fatigue, coughing fits, rheumatism, asthma, delirium tremens, migraine headaches, cramps, and depression associated with menstruation.

More recent research into the medical application of cannabis has shown that it is an effective analgesic, anti-inflammatory, anti-spasmodic and has proven beneficial in treating symptoms associated with:

- Multiple Sclerosis
- Glaucoma
- HIV and Aids
- Chemotherapy
- Cancer
- Arthritis
- Spinal Injuries

"Nearly all medicines have toxic, potentially lethal effects. But marijuana is not such a substance. There is no record in the extensive medical literature describing a proven, documented cannabis-induced fatality...Simply stated, researchers have been unable to give animals enough marijuana to induce death...In practical terms, marijuana cannot induce a lethal response as a result of drug-related toxicity...In strict medical terms, marijuana is far safer than many foods we commonly consume...Marijuana, in its natural form, is one of the safest therapeutically active substances known to man."

DEA Administrative Law Judge, FL Young, 1988.

Cannabis Cream

Many arthritis sufferers report that the application of a topical application to arthritic joints, twice a day aids with pain relief and reduces inflammation.

1 PINT HEMP OIL OR OLIVE OIL

2½ OZ (65G) BEESWAX

1½ OZ (40G) CANNABIS TRIM LEAVES

2 PINTS WATER

ESSENTIAL OIL OF LAVENDER (OPTIONAL)

Ideally, the cream should be made in a slow cooker; alternatively, a saucepan can be used. However, simmer only, DO NOT boil.

Add the oil, trim, and water together in your pan or slow cooker.

Simmer for 4 hours, stirring every 30 minutes or so.

After 4 hours, allow to cool.

Pour the contents of the pan/slow cooker through a sieve into a clean bowl or plastic container. Press the cannabis trim with the back of a spoon to force out as much oil as possible, then discard trim.

Place the water and oil solution into the coldest part of the fridge. After 24 to

48 hours (if your fridge is at the correct temperature) the oil infused with cannabis will solidify, which will allow you to separate the water from the oil. Discard the water.

Alternatively, the oil and water mix can be placed in a freezer and then separated.

You should now be left with a slightly green olive oil in solid form.

Place the green-tinged solid oil into a saucepan and gently heat. Simmer only, DO NOT boil.

When the oil has returned to a liquid state, add the beeswax (small pieces of wax will dissolve quicker than one big piece). Keep stirring until all the wax has dissolved. A few drops of essential oil of lavender can be added with the beeswax if you wish for a less "Canna" aroma.

Pour into suitable containers. Wide-necked jars or margarine tubs are best. Allow to cool.

Application of the cream twice a day (morning and evening) seems to produce the most favourable results.

Cannabis tincture

A cannabis tincture is simply an extract of cannabis in alcohol. It is easy to produce and very versatile.

The higher the alcohol content the better. Tinctures made with Everclear give very acceptable results. To increase the strength of the tincture, simply allow more alcohol to evaporate.

The cannabis tincture can be used by administering drops under the tongue or it can be dissolved into drink or food.

Finely chop $\frac{1}{2}$ oz (15g) cannabis bud and place in a wide-necked jam-jar or similar.

Cover it with alcohol and store in a dark and cool place for 2 weeks. Shake it every day.

After 2 weeks, filter the mixture using a coffee filter. Squeeze the last drops of alcohol out of the plant material.

Repeat this process again by adding a freshly chopped $\frac{1}{2}$ oz (15g) of cannabis.

The final stage is to increase the potency by reducing the volume of alcohol; this is achieved by evaporation.

Carefully pour the mixture onto a large, shallow plate, the large surface area will aid the evaporation process. As a guideline, evaporate two-thirds of the volume of alcohol and decanter the remainder into a small dropper bottle.

Top Tip

Do not be tempted to speed up the process by applying heat, as there is a strong risk of explosion

CANNABIS FAQ

If you've got questions about the use of marijuana, from how to get high to the long-term effects, then we've got the answers…

Q: Is it addictive?

A: There is little evidence to suggest that cannabis itself is physically addictive. Some would argue that there is a risk of mental addiction, where the mind finds it very hard to go without getting high, but this is normally seen in people who use it on a very regular basis. However, tobacco is incredibly addictive, both physically and mentally, due to its nicotine content. As most people smoke cannabis mixed with tobacco, there is some danger that an addiction will occur. Try to smoke pure marijuana, or mix it with a herbal smoking mixture which doesn't contain nicotine.

Q: How much should I use in a spliff?

A: Generally you require very little good weed or hash to get high; just a thin layer in a spliff will normally do, and $^1/_8$ oz (3.5g) will generally be enough for 10–15 joints. However, as the strength depends on the THC content, you will find you need to use more weed with a low THC content to get stoned. Be careful: some hydroponic strains are incredibly potent. One way to judge the potency before smoking (although it's not 100 per cent reliable) is to look for the amount of white THC crystals covering the weed—the more there are, the stronger it will be. A strong smell is not always a good indication of actual strength.

Q: What are the health risks?

A: Because of the illegal status of cannabis, research into the associated health risks is not as comprehensive as it should be. However, we know that smoking is bad, whatever you smoke, because it exposes your body to more than average levels of carcinogens and free radicals. Current medical thinking would suggest that smoking three pure joints a day is equivalent to 20 cigarettes, but this has been disputed, and light-to-moderate users are less likely to suffer than cigarette smokers. On the other hand, its stress-busting qualities are thought to be very beneficial to our well-being.

Q: What are the best ways to smoke it?

A: Most of the harmful byproducts of cannabis are released when it is burned, but many more can be filtered out with the use of a water bong. Smoking it pure (through a pipe or chillum) or with a herbal smoking mixture is far better than mixing it with tobacco (and the high is much cleaner and more intense). Possibly the best way to smoke it is by using a vaporizer, which heats up the cannabis until the active ingredient is vaporized for inhaling, but the plant material around it remains unburned and therefore the nasty chemicals are not released.

Q: Does eating it have a different effect?

A: Very much so. A good hash brownie is enough to reduce even the most hardened of smokers to a giggling wreck. One of the most common mistakes made when eating cannabis is not having the patience to let the high come on. When smoking, the THC can get working straight away, as the lungs offer it quick passage into the bloodstream and to the brain. When you eat cannabis, it has to be digested before it has an effect, so leave it a couple of hours before you decide whether to have another brownie or not.

Q: Can I be arrested for possession?

A: This depends where you are in the world. Most European countries are now tolerant to small amounts for personal use, but it is always best to check—even a small amount can land you in jail in Greece. The US is so fanatical about its drugs war that it would be foolish not to be incredibly careful about carrying the drug.

For more information about legality around the world, check out the Cannabis Campaigners Guide at www.ccguide.org.uk.

Q: Is cannabis just for getting high?

A: When you get stoned for the first time, the effect may seem to be unmanageable and counterproductive to anything you want to do. However, regular users can manage this effect and find that the mind-freeing result of cannabis is excellent for meditation, lateral thinking, and creative pursuits where the mind benefits from being less anchored.

Although its medical uses are slowly being investigated, there can be no doubt that it has an effect on a range of conditions from pain relief to increased mobility in MS sufferers.

The plant also makes excellent rope, paper, and cloth, to mention just a few of its additional uses.

Q: Will it affect my fertility?

A: Research in the US and Ireland suggests that heavy use makes sperm behave erratically, using up too much energy before reaching the egg and, more crucially, unable to digest the egg's outer layer when it gets there. However, research in this area is still limited, and certainly many marijuana smokers throughout history have had no problems fathering children.

Q: What should I expect when I first take it?

A: The effects you can expect are usually (in order): a slight tingling of the feet, numbness of extremities, an inability to stop smiling and giggling, an added dimension to colors, sound, smells, and other senses, a feeling of being separate from events around you, the munchies, and, finally, tiredness. This is only a rough guide, though, and not everyone experiences it this way. Non-smokers who smoke a joint for the first time tend to find the event a bit of a letdown because they either don't take the smoke into the lungs, or spend much of the time coughing.

GLOSSARY

Acidic
Acid, pH 6 or lower

Aeration
Supplying air or oxygen to root system

Aeroponics
Cultivating plants without a medium and supplying nutrient via a light misting or fine spray

Alkaline
pH 8 or higher

Booster
Feed high in phosphorus, used to increase yield

Bonsai
Small or dwarf plant

Botrytis
Fungal infection, commonly known as bud rot

Bud
Stem or branch containing dense calyxes

Calyx
Pod containing female ovule (seed pod), which has two protruding pistils

Chlorine
Chemical used to purify water

Chlorophyll
Gives plants their green color

Cola
Flowering top, a big bud or "main cola"

Clay pebble
Used as a medium

Cutting
Growing tip cut from a parent plant to produce a genetic copy of the host plant

Dioecious
Having male or female flowers

Dripper
Watering system that allows precise delivery of nutrients

Fan leaf
Large cannabis leaf, the "lungs" of the plant

Guano
Bird dung, which has very high organic nutrient content

Hashish
Pressed, solid form of cannabis

Hermie
Hermaphrodite, a plant having both male and female flowers

H.I.D.
High Intensity Discharge

HPS
High Pressure Sodium

Humidity
Measure of water held in the air

Hydroponics
Growing plants without soil in a liquid nutrient solution

Hygrometer
Instrument to measure relative humidity

Hypocotyl
Stem that appears from seed case

Internode
The point where side shoots develop

Kilowatt-hour
Amount of electricity consumed in one hour, e.g. a 1000w light will use one kilowatt in one hour

Leech
Heavy watering to remove build up of salts from medium

Lumen
Measure of light output

Manicure
Close trim of the buds

Marijuana
American term to describe cannabis

Mother
A female cannabis plant used to provide cuttings (clones)

NFT
Nutrient Film Technique

Ohm's Law
Volts multiplied by Amperes equals Watts

Ovule
Egg within the calyx, when pollinated will produce seed

Perlite
Heat-treated sand or volcanic glass used as a growing medium

pH
Scale of 1 to 14 measuring acidity and alkaline, pH 7 being neutral

Pistil
Small pair of hairs protruding from top of calyx, used to trap pollen

Pot Bound
Normal growth inhibited if the pot is too small for the root system

Resin
Pure form of hashish

Sinsemilla
Spanish for "without seed"

Stomata
Pores on the underside of leaves

THC
Tetrahydrocannabinol, the compound credited with producing a high

Trellis
A frame providing support

Trichome
Mushroom-shaped structure containing cannabinoids

Wick
Used in passive hydroponic systems to supply nutrients via capillary action

WEBSITES

There are more than a million sites devoted to cannabis. The following are as good a starting point as any and provide gateway links to many others.

www.cannabis.com
www.cannabisculture.com
www.cannabisnews.com
www.drugslibrary.org
www.hightimes.com
www.everyonedoesit.com
www.budbuddies.com
www.uk420.com
www.just-green.com

PICTURE CREDITS

All images copyright Anova Books except the following:

Owen Franken/Corbis	7
Corbis	10, 107
Rex Features	11
Romeo Ranoco/Reuters	12
EveryoneDoesIT.com	14
David Strange	16, 30, 34, 35, 37, 43 (t), 47, 52, 56, 57 (r), 59, 73, 79, 91, 92, 95 (l & b), 96
Jeff Ditchfield	21 (r), 51, 57 (l), 60 (t), 100, 101 (all), 108
UK420.com	28, 32 (all), 33, 36, 54 (l), 55 (r), 64 (b)
www.just-green.com	94 (all)
SAKKI	98

ACKNOWLEDGMENTS

My fee for this book has been donated to the cannabis cultivation site www.uk420.com for a fund that will be used to promote and assist medicinal cannabis groups in the UK.

I would like to thank all the growers and stoners who have assisted with, and contributed to, this book. Special thanks to my friend Laurence Brierley for the inspiration to set up Bud Buddies.

And a thank you to the following www.uk420.com members:

MS?MJ!
Oldtimer1
Joolz
maryjane
Red dragon
Grim Reefer
Lungs
OMH
BushBandicoot
Kafka
Kali Man
Thefugitive
HvyFuel
Danzig

www.just-green.com

Spiritual guidance was received from the Reverend Paul Farnhill of The Cannabis Assembly

www.budbuddies.com—the medical cannabis co-operative